Elisabeth Stuart is Area Archivist at the ᵥₑₑ
Plymouth and has lived in Devon for the past ten years. Born and
brought up in Surrey, her favourite pursuit is travelling abroad,
particularly in France. During the early part of 1988, she spent most of
her weekends visiting various parishes in Devon where she found many
more Curiosities than it was possible to include in this book. From her
home in Stonehouse, Plymouth, she can swim in the sea before
breakfast in summer, whilst enjoying magnificent walks along the
South West coastal footpaths at all times of the year.

Frontispiece
The Charge of the Light Brigade Monument, Hatherleigh
(see No. 51)

Devon Curiosities

Elisabeth Stuart

Line Drawings by Chris Robinson

THE DOVECOTE PRESS

In memory of my grandmother, Irene Benn (1882-1974),
who knew how to make life fun.

First published in 1989 by The Dovecote Press Ltd
Stanbridge, Wimborne, Dorset BH21 4JD

ISBN 0 946159 53 X

Photoset in Times by Character Graphics, Taunton, Somerset
Printed and bound by Biddles Ltd, Guildford and King's Lynn

Contents

Introduction

The English countryside is a palimpsest, and what more enjoyable way of spending a day then exploring it. Devon is particularly rewarding in this respect, because less intensive use of the land available has meant that many places have retained their *genius loci*, unlike, say, the crowded south-east of England where it is much rarer, though by no means impossible, to come across curiosities.

This book is intended for the general reader, and the text does not purport to be based on original research; rather, most of the effort went into research on the ground, a delight for anyone whose days are normally spend desk-bound! So often, well-known places are over-run by tourists when a short distance away lies something equally if not more interesting to visit.

One of the best bits about writing this book has been the support of many friends. In particular, I should mention John and Jane Somers Cocks, whose unfailing resourcefulness and constant encouragement have been particularly welcome. William Leedham, Jeremy Pearson, Peter Hamilton and Colin Kilvington have each helped me in different ways. Other people have been kind enough to respond to my letters, arriving often out of the blue. In my researches on the ground at weekends, virtually every farm I have visited offered hospitality in the form of a cup of tea. Mr Michael Lee of Dowrich and the owner of Mohun's Ottery deserve particular thanks for allowing me to include their gatehouses.

Anybody exploring the Devon landscape owes an enormous debt to Professor WG Hoskins. In preparing the text, *Devon and Cornwall Notes and Queries* proved a useful quarry. I also owe thanks to Louise Rose of the North Devon Record Office in Barnstaple for transcribing the passage quoted in No 52, and to the staff of the Local Studies and Reference Library in Plymouth, Plymouth City Museum and Art Gallery, Royal Albert Memorial Museum, Devon Record Office and West Country Studies Library in Exeter. The staff of Computerbase, Plymouth, gave valuable help in mastering the complexities of my word-processor, and I am equally indebted to Chris Robinson for providing such delightful line-drawings to accompany the other illustrations.

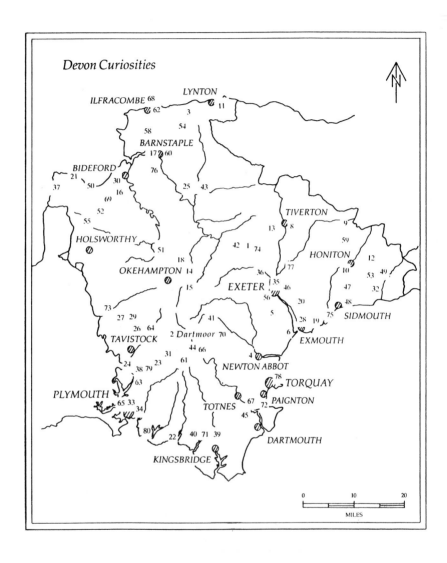

Devon Curiosities

ILFRACOMBE ⁶⁸
62
LYNTON
11
3
58
54
BARNSTAPLE
17 60
BIDEFORD
21
50
30
69
16
76
25
43
37
52
55
TIVERTON
13
8
9
HOLSWORTHY
51
42 1 74
59
18
HONITON
12
OKEHAMPTON 14
36
77
10
53
49
15
EXETER
35
46
47
32
56
20
48
73
5
28 19
75
SIDMOUTH
27 29
41
6
26 64
2 Dartmoor 70
TAVISTOCK
44 66
EXMOUTH
31
24
38 79 23
61
4
63
NEWTON ABBOT
PLYMOUTH
78
TORQUAY
65 33
34
67 72
PAIGNTON
TOTNES
45
80
22
40 71 39
DARTMOUTH
KINGSBRIDGE

0   10   20

MILES

1 The Cockstride Ghost, Lewis Dowrich of Sandford

Position: Sandford
Ordnance Map: Okehampton and North Dartmoor Sheet 191 1:50,000
Map Ref: SS 8280/0510
Access: From Crediton, take the road through Sandford and continue
to Dowrich Bridge. Dowrich gatehouse is up the track on the left,
marked 'private' but the owner has kindly given permission for visitors
to look at the gatehouse.

Note: Lewis Dowrich of Sandford, returning home after a convivial
evening drinking brandy-punch at the house of a friend, fell off his
horse at Dowrich Bridge in 1717, and was buried on September 17.
Opinion varies as to whether he had died of a broken neck or was
drowned, but legend has it that since that date his spirit has been
gradually moving up the hill towards Dowrich House by a 'cockstride'
in every month. A 'cockstride' is reckoned to be about six inches. Since
ghosts have to return to their resting-place at dawn (cockcrow), Lewis's
spirit moves fairly fast: most cockstride ghosts are limited to a
cockstride a year. However, he is not allowed to use the road, but
rather a bridge 'as narrow and sharp as the edge of a sword, unrolling
itself as he advances'. Should he fall off, he must return to the stream

and start again.

Fears that the cockstride ghost might be able to climb up the steps leading to the gatehouse prevented one owner from adding an additional bottom step to the gatehouse. However, on Friday September 7 1973, part of the wall at the side of the gatehouse was taken down, and a gardener cutting the grass in front of Dowrich House saw a man in a long black coat and cape sitting on a black horse and holding a silver whip in his right hand.

Could this have been Lewis Dowrich?

Local Places of Interest
   42. The Copstone, Copplestone
   74. Sandford School
Food and Accommodation
   Available in Sandford and Crediton

The Powdermills, Postbridge

2 Powdermills, Postbridge

Position: Postbridge
Ordnance Map: Okehampton and North Dartmoor Sheet 191 1:50,000
Map Ref: SX 6275/7735
Access: The powdermills lie on the left-hand side of the B3212 running
from Two Bridges to Postbridge, soon after the Cherrybrook Hotel.

Note: These mills were erected in 1844 by Alderman George Frean of
Plymouth under the patronage of Prince Albert (who had married
Queen Victoria in 1840). The gunpowder produced could be used
either for gunnery or for blasting operations, particularly land
clearance. Much of the gunpowder was used at the Delabole slate
quarries in Cornwall. A 'recipe' of 1797 suggests 70 parts of nitre
(another name for saltpetre), 18 parts of sulphur and 16 parts of
charcoal. These elements had to be ground up before the powder could
be tested by firing from the bombard or mortar which lies on the left
hand side as you come down the drive. This might be dangerous on
occasions, hence the choice of such an isolated spot on Dartmoor.

The mills stand close to water which would have provided the energy
for these operations. Unfortunately, Alderman Frean failed to obtain a
licence from the Duchy of Cornwall, which owns much of Dartmoor, to
cut the leat or water-channel near the mills, although leats were later
built (and can still be seen) from the Cherry Brook and East Dart. The
mills became obsolescent about forty years after they had been built
due to the exploitation of an alternative explosive, dynamite, which
had been invented in 1867.

Local Places of Interest
    31. Childe's Tomb, Dartmoor
    41. Moretonhampstead Almshouses
    61. Dartmoor Letter-box, Ducks' Pool
Food and Accommodation
    The East Dart Hotel, Postbridge

3 The Musicians' Gallery

Position: At the back of old Parracombe Church
Ordnance Map: Barnstaple and Ilfracombe Sheet 180 1:50,000
Map Ref: SS 6745/4495
Access: Parracombe village lies just off the left-hand side of the A39
running from Blackmoor Gate towards Lynton. Go through
Parracombe (the new church is on your right) and take the road on
your right towards Churchtown.

Note: Two hundred years ago, church music was often provided by a
band of musicians. A typical church band might include violin, clarinet
and bass viol, though sometimes a flute or bassoon replaced the violin.
St Petrock's church, Parracombe, may have been the last Devon
church to keep up this tradition. In any case, the musicians' gallery still
survives among the box-pews at the back of the church; part of one pew
has actually been removed to allow space for someone playing the bass
viol in the pew behind. The choir would have sat in the gallery too. In
some parishes, the band would perform outside people's houses at
Christmas as the 'Waits'; the money collected in this way would be used
to sustain the choir throughout the coming year.

Like Molland church, also in North Devon, Parracombe church still
has its three-decker pulpit, including a reading desk for the minister
and seat for the parish clerk. Both also have a screen dividing the nave
from the chancel on which are recorded the Ten Commandments.

St Petrock's is now redundant. In 1879, people became worried that
the church was unsafe, and it was resolved to pull it down, erecting a
new church on the site. However, a body of protesters led by the
author, artist and social reformer John Ruskin (1819-1900) persuaded
the authorities to choose a fresh site in the village for the new church in
order to save St Petrock's. Ruskin would have been about sixty at this
date. Although a rich man himself, much of his life's work was
concerned with bringing art into the lives of people less wealthy,
particularly the working classes. He believed that 'the highest wisdom
and the highest treasure need not be costly or exclusive', and in 1854-58
had organized a series of drawing classes at the Working Men's
College, Great Ormond Street, London. He was also a friend of many
painters and defender of the Pre-Raphaelites, and in 1870-79 and 1883-
84 was the first Slade Professor of Art at Oxford University, so his
views would have carried weight in a number of circles.

Despite its remote position on Exmoor, and the fact that church
services are no longer held there regularly (burials continued until

[12]

1971), St Petrock's arouses great affection and is one of the most frequently visited churches in the country.

Local Places of Interest
54. Arlington Granary
Food and Accommodation
The Fox and Goose Inn, Parracombe

4 Puritans' Pit, Bradley Woods

Position: Newton Abbot
Ordnance Map: Torbay and South Dartmoor Sheet 202 1:50,000
Map Ref: SX 8440/7090
Access: Take the A381 Totnes Road out of Newton Abbot. Fork left
up Old Totnes road, take the first right turn into Bradley Road and
park. Cross the A381 and take the path immediately to the left of the
terrace of modern houses. Follow this through the wood to the River
Lemon on your right and on a little way. The Pit is above the path
before the Mill is reached.

Note: Puritans' Pit is a collapsed limestone cavern where William Yeo,
the 17th century Puritan minister ejected from his parish of
Wolborough for refusal to observe the Act of Uniformity, preached by
night to his parishioners. Despite the price on his head (£2), he
managed to avoid being caught until the religous climate had changed,
and the Nonconformist chapel was built at 51 Wolborough Street,
Newton Abbot. He died in 1699 aged 82.

'Puritans' were so called because they wanted their services to be
free of any taint of Catholicism: no ornament, no robes, no music. Such
a form of worship had considerable appeal for English middle-class
merchants.

During the reign of Elizabeth I (1558-1603), Puritans attempted to
remain within the established church and set up secret presbyteries.
However, soon after James I's accession in 1603, the Hampton Court
Conference, prompted by a Puritan petition, made it clear that this
would not be possible. All clergy were expected to conform or leave.
As a result, many Puritans emigrated to Holland or the New World.

Not till the outbreak of the Civil War in 1642 did the Puritans achieve
power, and when this happened, they found it impossible to agree.
After Cromwell's regime began in 1649, they split up into sects.

After the Restoration, Puritans went underground because they
were so unpopular, gradually emerging as Nonconformists. After the
advent of William of Orange in 1688, whom they had supported, they
had the right to have their own churches, hence the Nonconformist
chapel referred to above.

Local Places of Interest
    44. Ten Commandments Stone, Buckland Beacon
    66. My Dear Mother Clock, Buckland-in-the-Moor
Food and Accommodation
    Plenty available in Newton Abbot

5 The Lawrence Tower, Dunchideock

Position: Dunchideock near Exeter
Ordnance Map: Exeter, Sidmouth and surrounding area Sheet 192
1:50,000
Map Ref: SX 8750/8610
Access: Turn off the A38 running between Ashburton and Exeter
towards Dunchideock. The Belvedere tower lies on the right-hand side
after going through the forest road towards Dunchideock.

Note: This folly, on a commanding site on Haldon Hill, was named
Lawrence Castle by its builder Sir Robert Palk, who erected it in 1788
in memory of the man who had made him his heir, Major General
Stringer Lawrence. Lawrence (1697-1775) had sailed out to India to

fight, but was captured by the French – although he was soon released when peace was concluded between the rival French and British powers in 1748. He rose in rank from lieutenant-colonel in 1754, to be brigadier-general in 1757 and major-general by 1759. He was nicknamed 'father of the Indian Army'. There is another memorial to Lawrence in Dunchideock church:

'Major General Stringer Lawrence
Who commanded in India
From 1747 to 1767
Died 10th Jan 1775 aged 78
The Desperate State of Affairs in India
becoming prosperous by a Series of Victories
endeared him to his Country.
History has recorded his Fame
The Regrets of the Worthy bear
Testimony to his Virtues
Born to Command, to conquer and to Spare,
As Mercy mild, yet terrible as War,
Here LAWRENCE rests; the Trump of honest Fame
From Thames to Ganges has proclaimed his Name
In vain this frail Memorial Friendship rears,
His Dearest Monuments an Army's tears;
His Deeds on fairer Columns stand engrav'd
In Provinces preserved and Cities sav'd.

Sir Robert Palk (1717-98) became a member of the Madras Council in 1753, and Governor from 1763-67; he was responsible for making the peace of Hyderabad in 1766, and returned to this country a year later. He was to become MP for Ashburton, and was created first baronet in 1772.

The Tower is privately owned, but a board giving opening times is posted at the entrance.

Local Places of Interest
    6. Mamhead Obelisk
Food and Accommodation
    The Nobody Inn, Doddiscombsleigh

6 Mamhead Obelisk

Position: Mamhead Woods
Ordnance Map: Exeter, Sidmouth and surrounding area Sheet 192
1:50,000
Map Ref: SX 9250/8065
Access: Take the B3381 off the A380 running from Kingsteignton to
Kennford. Take the minor road on your right until you see the car-park
on your left. Park car and walk through the wood (there is a signboard
showing the obelisk).

Note: From the obelisk are marvellous views over the Exe estuary. It
was built in either 1742 or 1743 by Thomas Ball (1671-1749), a
merchant, 'out of a regard to the safety of such as might use to sail out
of the Port of Exon or any others who might be driven on the coast'.

Thomas had succeeded to the estate in 1718, inheriting a house built by his grandfather Sir Peter Ball (1598-1680), attorney-general to Queen Henrietta Maria and his father. On his travels in Europe, Thomas collected rare trees with which he adorned Mamhead Park.

At the time it was built, the 100-foot high obelisk stood above the house, but in 1830 a Mr Newman employed the architect Anthony Salvin to build him a new house on a different site. Salvin (1799-1881), a pupil of John Nash, practised in London but was frequently employed to work on castles and country seats.

Local Places of Interest
   5. Lawrence Tower, Dunchideock
Food and Accommodation
   The Ship Inn, Cockwood

The Daymark, Dartmouth

7 The Daymark at Dartmouth Harbour Entrance

Position: Kingswear side of Dartmouth Harbour
Ordnance Map: Torbay and South Dartmoor Sheet 202 1:50,000
Map Ref: SX 9035/5028
Access: Take the B3205 from Brixham then turn left towards Coleton Fishacre (National Trust). At the crossroads at the entrance to Coleton Fishacre turn right, until you reach a car-park, also on your left, from which you can walk to the Daymark.

Note: This curious granite tower was built in 1864 by the Dart Harbour Commissioners. For centuries there had been a chapel to help guide sailors into the harbour entrance which is difficult to see from a vessel and can be treacherous due to the wind blowing in and out of the hills, and the ebb of the tide. The hills rise high on this Kingswear side of the harbour entrance. The tower is octagonal and is 80 foot high; it would only be useful in daytime.

Local Places of Interest
　　45. The Gatehouse to Cornworthy Priory
　　67. Galmpton Warborough Windmill
Food and Accommodation
　　Dartmouth

8 18th-19th Century Carvings, Blundell's School

Position: Tiverton, eastern edge of the town where it is approached by the B3391
Ordnance Map: Minehead and Brendon Hills area Sheet 181 1:50,000
Map Ref: SS 9575/1245

Note: Peter Blundell of Tiverton was a wool merchant who rose from humble beginnings. Two years before he died in 1601, he drafted a will making provision for a school of 150 boys (he had never married so presumably had no children of his own!). The school was intended for children 'born or for the most parte before their age of sixe years brought upp in the towne or parrish of Tyverton aforesaid'. In 1839, it was suggested this be modified since only 29 boys fell into this category.

The school was the subject of some controversy in that year. Some of the local gentry and merchants felt the school should expand its curriculum to take in literature and science besides the Classics. Another faction was against this. Many Devon boys at this time were entering the army and navy, and the school also provided candidates for the East India Company.

The original school hall built in 1604 still stands and boys in the eighteenth and nineteenth century have carved their names on the front. When he wrote his will, Peter Blundell had given strict instructions about this 'faier School House to conteyne for the place for teaching only in length one hundred foote and in breadth fower and twenty foot, a hawle, buttery and kitchin . . . with fit and convenient roomes over the same hawle, buttery and kitchin, all the windows well and strongly glassed and barred with iron barrs, the floor of the school to be well plancked with plancks of oke etc'. The cupola was added in 1740.

Local Places of Interest
13. The Revolving Lych-Gate, Cruwys Morchard
Food and Accommodation
Plenty available in Tiverton. Also The Swan Inn at Bampton

9 Plaque to the Murder of William Blackmore, Clayhidon

Position: Clayhidon
Ordnance Map: Taunton and Lyme Regis Sheet 193 1:50,000
Map Ref: ST 1635/1410
Access: From Clayhidon village (pub and church), follow the road south; at the crossroads, turn left and follow the road down the hill; the plaque is after the bridge on the right hand side of the road just before the next crossroads (road from Hemyock to Churchstanton).

Note: An iron plaque by the side of the road tells this grim tale: 'William Blackmore landsurveyor of Clayhidon Mills was murdered on this spot the 6th day of February 1853 by George Sparks of this parish who was executed at Exeter for the horrid crime'.
  Blackmore had been collecting his fees and on his way home stopped

at the White Horse Inn at Bolham, north of Tiverton. There he talked to two farm labourers called Sparkes and Hitchcock whose master had recently paid him. Drinking until after midnight, the labourers followed him back but shortly before he reached home, George Sparkes attacked him with a large pair of tongs and killed him. However, Sparkes was caught, tried and executed in front of a crowd of several thousand people at the County Prison, Exeter on April 1st.

Land-surveying was a profession which grew up in the sixteenth century. At the beginning, surveyors had a bad reputation because many were not properly qualified. Ralph Agas, a contemporary, jested 'Marry, he was a plumber, and had learned from a painter'. However, others could see the practical usefulness of their activities: another contemporary, Aaron Rathbone, put their comments into verse

'Both simple, gentle, Barons, Lords and Knights
Will take thee for their chiefest of delights
Thou teachest them to measure all their grounde
Which, certainly, will save them many a pound'.

Many fine estate maps were produced by surveyors in the seventeenth and eighteenth centuries, whilst in the nineteenth century legislation such as the General Enclosure Acts of 1836 and 1845, and the Tithe Commutation Act of 1836 provided them with plenty of work.

Local Places of Interest
   59. Mohun's Ottery Gatehouse, Luppitt
Food and Accommodation
   Available in local pubs

10 Tom Putt's Beech Avenue

Position: Gittisham
Ordnance Map: Exeter, Sidmouth and surrounding area Sheet 192
1:50,000
Map Ref: SY 1470/9845
Access: Take the road running east out of Gittisham village towards the
A375.

Note: Tom Putt was a Bencher of the Middle Temple after whom a
variety of apple was named. The low-spreading Tom Putt is still grown
in some West Country orchards, and was once much prized as a
cooking apple. Born on 27 December 1722, his family lived at Coombe
House, Gittisham (now a country house hotel) for nearly 200 years.
Tom married Elizabeth Newton of Tiverton but died at Gittisham
without any children on 4 April 1787. He was succeeded by his brother
William, who was Vicar of Gittisham from 1753 until his death. Tom's
waistcoat is now in Topsham Museum (Curiousity No 20).
    Tom planted a beech avenue on Gittisham Hill, which is very fine.

Local Places of Interest
    47. The Whistling Cock, Ottery St Mary
Food and Accommodation
    Coombe House Hotel, Gittisham

11 The Rhenish Tower, Lynmouth

Position: Lynmouth main street facing the sea
Ordnance Map: Barnstaple and Ilfracombe Sheet 180 1:50,000
Map Ref: SS 7230/4950

Note: The original Rhenish Tower was built in the late 1850's by a
General Rawdon who intended to keep salt-water there for use in baths
in his house. In 1860 he further refined it by adding battlements.
Rawdon is said to have chosen the design from a painting in a friend's
house. In 1905, a contemporary guide to the town noted that a hundred
candle power electric beam shone from the tower to lead vessels safely
to the harbour.

    However, the original tower was destroyed in the Lynmouth flood of
15-16 August 1952 and the present building is a copy. 31 people were
killed in the floods, and over 90 houses irreparably damaged.

Local Places of Interest
   3. Musicians' Gallery, Parracombe
Food and Accommodation
   Plenty available locally

12 Loughwood Meeting House, Dalwood

Position: Dalwood
Ordnance Map: Exeter, Sidmouth and surrounding area Sheet 192
1:50,000
Map Ref: SY 2530/9925
Access: Take the A35(T) out of Honiton towards Bridport. Dalwood
lies on the left-hand side of the road between Wilmington and
Kilmington; however, your easiest approach is to take the turning to
Loughwood Farm, and follow the steep road to the bottom.
Loughwood Chapel lies near the farm.

Note: The meeting house was begun on 14 December 1653 and finished
the following August. It was intended for the use of Baptists who were
not allowed to meet officially for worship at this date. The site was ideal
because it was in the middle of a wood, which has since been felled. An
apochryphal story tells that on one occasion a huntsman was found in
the pulpit, his hounds in the pews! The meeting house has two small
rooms at the back of the place of worship, intended as living rooms for
the pastor.

Two possible founders of the Loughwood Baptists were soldiers
from Cromwell's army: John Vernon and William Allen. They came to
Axminster after the Battle of Naseby in 1645 and wed the daughters of
James Huish of Sidbury. Vernon wrote a book called *The Young*

Horseman, intended for men in the Parliamentary Cavalry schooling their horses.

A colourful figure here in the 18th century was Reverend Isaac Hann, pastor from 1747-78. He married Grace Haddon in 1720, and they lived at Popain Dalwood. The Western Association of Preachers records admiringly on its tablet

> 'Wit sparkled in his pleasing face, with zeal his heart was fired
> Few ministers so humble were, yet few so much admir'd
> Ripen'd for heaven by grace divine like autumn fruit he fell
> Reader! think not to live as long, but seek to live as well!'

The meeting house was renovated and reopened in 1871.

Local Places of Interest
49. Axminster Carpet Factory
53. Shute Gatehouse
Food and Accommodation
Plenty available in Axminster. The White Cottage Restaurant, Honiton

The revolving lych-gate, Cruwys Morchard

13 The Revolving Lych-Gate, Cruwys Morchard

Position: Cruwys Morchard church
Ordnance Map: Minehead and Brendon Hills area Sheet 181 1:50,000
Map Ref: SS 8745/1220

Note: Cruwys Morchard lych-gate is unusual because its double gates revolve around a central pivot.

The earliest record of a lych-gate in this country is in 1482. It was intended as the gateway to a church, and had a roof so that the corpse ('lich') could be set down to await the clergyman's arrival. When he came, he would read the introductory part of the service before preceding the funeral train into the church.

The Saxon word 'lic' or 'lice', meaning a body, has given rise to the Gothic 'leik', Dutch 'lijk', Danish 'lig', Swedish 'lik' and German 'leiche' and Old High German 'lih'. It means form or shape or as we might say, likeness. Hence a variety of words 'lich owl' or screech owl, so called because its sound was thought to mean impending death in the house; 'lich wake' meaning a vigil with the dead; 'lich field' meaning field of dead bodies; and 'lich way' meaning the path by which the dead were carried to the grave.

The name Cruwys Morchard is derived from Celtic and means Great ('mor') wood ('coed' hence orchard). Alexander de Crues held the manor in 1242.

Local Places of Interest
   8. 18-19th century Carvings at Blundell's School, Tiverton
Food and Accommodation
   Plenty available in Tiverton

14 The White Bird of the Oxenhams

Position: South Tawton church has Oxenham memorials
Ordnance Map: Okehampton and North Dartmoor Sheet 191 1:50,000
Map Ref: SX 6530/9445

Note: Memorials in South Tawton church to the Oxenham family draw attention to their existence in this parish from the 13th until the early 19th century.

Legend relates that when a member of the family was about to die, a white bird resembling a thrush but with a couple of horns on its head would appear. The bird was much like the charadrius or caladrius often depicted in medieval manuscripts derived from the Bible. Should the bird regard the dying person, he or she would recover because it would draw the illness to itself. But if it ignored the patient and looked away, there was no hope.

Symbolically, it represents Christ who is free from all sin. It was believed that just as Christ turned away His face from the Jews because they did not believe in Him, and turned towards the Gentiles, taking their frailties upon Him, so did the bird.

Sabine Baring-Gould (Curiosity No 27) questioned this tale, on the grounds that in one instance the bird was said to have appeared to members of the family at Zeal Monachorum, a neighbouring parish. However, Professor Hoskins has pointed out that there were members of the Oxenham family who lived at Zeal Monachorum. The bird has apparently made its appearance to no fewer than 14 Oxenhams between 1618-1892; four of these occurrences were in 1635.

Outside South Tawton church is a small oak planted there in 1984 to replace an elm which is said to have stood there since 1688 and which recently died of Dutch elm disease.

Local Places of Interest
15. St Mary's Chapel, South Zeal
Food and Accommodation
The Oxenham Arms, South Zeal

15 St Mary's Chapel, South Zeal

Position: South Zeal
Ordnance Map: Okehampton and North Dartmoor Sheet 191 1:50,000
Map Ref: SX 6509/9360
Access: In the centre of South Zeal village, towards the top of the hill.

Note: This site was probably originally used for a weavers' guild chapel.
The present granite built chapel is said to date from 1713, although
Pevsner has questioned this, pointing out that its style is completely
pre-classical. He suggests that it may have been restored in 1713.
Whenever it was built, it functioned as a school from 1773 until 1877
when it was converted to a chapel of ease for South Tawton. Chapels of
ease were built for the use of those parishioners who lived at some
distance from the church itself. Since South Tawton lies on the
northern edge of Dartmoor, we can imagine that this might have been
very useful on occasions.

Near the chapel in one direction stands a fine medieval market cross,

and in another direction lies the Oxenham Arms. This building probably dates from the early 16th century and was built around a menhir. The word 'menhir' is derived from 'men' meaning stone and 'hir' meaning long. The present hotel, which at one time belonged to the Oxenham family (Curiosity No 14), has a distinguished literary past. Charles Dickens (1812-70) is said to have been caught in a snowstorm here and used the time profitably to write part of the *Pickwick Papers* in 1836.

The chapel is described in Eden Philpotts's novel *The Beacon*, written in 1928: 'In the midst of Zeal rose a graceful cross above four crooked steps. It lifted with a long stalk and short arms, and the road divided here to right and left, leaving the cross and an open space and a little chapel together in the midst. A shining clock beamed from the chapel, and the hands moved over golden figures; while above, two exposed bells hung together in a tiny turret, and at times twittered thinly like birds, to call the people to prayer.'

Local Places of Interest
14. The White Bird of the Oxenhams, South Tawton
Food and Accommodation
The Oxenham Arms, South Zeal

16 A Medieval Prophylactic, Weare Giffard

Position: In Weare Giffard church
Ordnance Map: Barnstaple and Ilfracombe Sheet 180 1:50,000
Map Ref: SS 4610/2210
Access: Take the road running north-west out of Great Torrington to Weare Giffard.

Note: As chief patron of the arts at a time when the majority of people were illiterate, it is not surprising that the medieval church in Western Europe often used wall painting as a medium for the message. Medieval builders expected the walls to be painted, and only after the Reformation were these pictures white-washed.

Opinions differ as to whether the saint in process of being martyred in the wall-painting on the south wall of the church at Weare Giffard is St Edmund or St Sebastian. Both saints were shot to death by arrows, but whereas St Edmund was then beheaded, St Sebastian recovered and had to be beaten to death! In other respects, their lives were very different. Edmund (841-69) was a Saxon who was reared as a Christian and, as King of East Anglia, led his men against the Viking invaders in 869. He was killed at Hellesdon in Norfolk after being captured but refusing to submit or to abjure his religion; some accounts say he was not shot by arrows, but rather spreadeagled as a sacrifice. In either case, when his body was found in the early 10th century, it was incorrupt and was moved to the place which later became Bury St Edmunds, the seat of a great abbey.

St Sebastian, on the other hand, was a soldier in the army of the Roman emperor Diocletian about the year 283. Diocletian was so incensed at Sebastian's Christianity that he gave instructions for him to be killed. In the Middle Ages, St Sebastian was believed to be the patron saint against plague, possibly because he had been effective in curing someone of plague in one instance, or because of his fortitude in withstanding the arrows launched through the air. Plague was believed to be airborne at that time, so it was felt this saint might act as a defender against all dangers coming through the air. It has been suggested that this is the reason why the painting is above the priest's door, since the priest must often have had to deliver the Last Rites to the dying.

Local Places of Interest
  30. Bideford Bridge   52. John Abbot of Frithelstock
  69. Taddiport Chapel, Great Torrington

17 Spanish Merchants' House, Barnstaple

Position: Barnstaple
Ordnance Map: Barnstaple and Ilfracombe Sheet 180 1:50,000
Map Ref: SS 5595/3300
Access: No 62 Boutport Street is now the Woolwich Building Society, and lies near the Royal and Fortescue Hotel a short distance east of the bridge.

Note: The magnificent coat of arms in what is now the Woolwich Building Society is that of the Guild of Spanish Merchants who owned the house in the 17th century. This may be the origin of a payment among the borough accounts of 'xxs to Mr Allexander horwood and Mr Richard Ferris Rydinge to Exceter about the Spanish Companye'. The coat of arms may have been sculpted by John Abbot (Curiosity No 52).

The other coat of arms is that of Barnstaple Town Council. At one time, this was the town house of the Earls of Bath.

The house later became the Golden Lion Hotel and in 1823-24 the North Devon Telegraph coach began its journey to London from outside the house at 8 o'clock each morning except Sunday.

Local Places of Interest
  60. Queen Anne's Walk, Barnstaple
  76. Tawstock Gatehouse
Food and Accommodation
  Royal and Fortescue Hotel, Barnstaple

18 Church House, Sampford Courtenay

Position: Sampford Courtenay, just in front of the church
Ordnance Map: Okehampton and North Dartmoor Sheet 191 1:50,000
Map Ref: SX 6320/0129
Access: Sampford Courtenay lies just north of the A3072 between
Exbourne and North Tawton

Note: Sampford Courtenay Church House is where the Western or
Prayer Book Rebellion broke out in 1549. On Whitsunday, June 9th,
the new Prayer Book in English was introduced for the first time

according to the Act of Uniformity. Whether or not the parish priest compounded the distress of his parishioners by wearing the new surplice is uncertain, but in any case they were so unhappy with this 'Christmas game' that next day they forced the priest to revert to the traditional Latin Mass.

Local JPs would not tolerate this, however, and William Hellyons, a gentleman, upset the parishioners so much that a farmer attacked him as he climbed down the steps of the Church House. The rest of the mob lynched him, and so began the Rebellion which was not put down until mid-August.

Church houses, or church house inns, of which many survive in Devon, had a useful function combining business with pleasure. Church ales, the drink being provided by the churchwardens, were used to raise money for church expenses. There were variations on this theme: for instance, 'Bid Ales' to raise money for those temporarily in dire straits, 'Bride Ales' for newly wed couples and 'Clerk Ales' for the parish clerk. After 1603, church ales and similar activities were forbidden by a canon.

The Court Room upstairs in the Church House can sometimes be visited by obtaining the key from the house on the left. It was so called because at one time manor courts were held there, although later it was used as a poor house and, in the 19th century, as a school. A massive oak table and benches, its original furniture, remain within the Court Room.

Local Places of Interest
14. The White Bird of the Oxenhams, South Tawton
15. St Mary's Chapel, South Zeal
Food and Accommodation
The George Hotel, Hatherleigh

19 Joan Raleigh's Tomb, East Budleigh

Position: In East Budleigh church
Ordnance Map: Exeter, Sidmouth and surrounding area Sheet 192
1:50,000
Map Ref: SY 0660/8490
Access: Free car park below the church: to gain access, turn right off
the main village street running down the hill from the church. Free
public lavatories.

Note: East Budleigh church has a magnificent collection of carved
bench ends depicting motifs and characters from the early 16th century
when they were made.

In the centre aisle, covered by a rug, is the tombstone of Joan
Raleigh, first wife of Walter Raleigh, the father of Sir Walter Raleigh
(1552?-1618), the favourite of Queen Elizabeth I. The inscription on
the stone has been much worn away by generations of feet but it
appears that it was intended to read 'ORATE PRO AIA [ANIMA]
JOHANNE RALEYH UXRS [UXORIS] WALTRI [WALTERI] RALE
ARMIG [ARMIGERI] QUE OBIIT X DIE MENSI IUNII ANO [ANNO] D'
[Pray for the soul of Joan Raleigh, wife of Walter Raleigh, Esq, who

died the tenth day of the month of June, Anno Domini']. However the carver's ignorance or illiteracy was such that he carved it back to front! Because the tombstone was laid in such a central position, it is likely that the Raleigh family paid highly for this privilege. However, the incised stone slab, which is decorated with a cross known as a 'Latin cross fleurée', was simply a cheaper version of an engraved brass.

The Raleigh family home, Hayes Barton, can be reached by following the lane beyond the car park below the churchyard. It can be viewed from the outside. The Raleigh family pew in the church bears the date 1537.

Local Places of Interest
28. A La Ronde, Exmouth
75. The Brick Cross, Bicton
Food and Accommodation
The Globe Inn, Lympstone

20 The Pintleless Patent Rudder

Position: In the Museum, the Strand, Topsham
Ordnance Map: Exeter, Sidmouth and surrounding area Sheet 192
1:50,000
Map Ref: SX 9680/8765

Note: 'All practical men engaged in the building or navigation of ships
know that one of their great safety valves is the security of the Rudder
. . Having been at sea 25 years and above 20 years engaged as
Surveyor for Lloyds, I have had considerable experience in the
building and equipment of ships. I suffered great loss and
inconvenience some time ago, by 2 ships breaking their Rudders'. So
wrote John Bagwell Holman (1800-63). Clearly, he was a practical man
because he set out to do something about the problem and invented the
Pintleless Patent Rudder, which could be removed under water and
brought up to be mended. An example of this is kept in Topsham
Museum, established in 1967 in a former sail-loft by his great-
granddaughter, Dorothy Holman.

John Bagwell Holman began as a marine insurer. Previously, there
had been little provision for ship insurance until he began the Mutual
West of England Marine Insurance Association in 1832; from 1839-63,
he acted as Lloyds Surveyor for Topsham and Devon. In 1842, he took
over an existing ship-building firm in Topsham, which he developed
together with his five sons. In 30 years (1849-79), they constructed as
many as 31 ships and a painting in the museum shows the Tor Fleet,
each flying the Holman flag, owned by the family.

Topsham was important from the early 17th century for ship-
building. However, by the late 19th century, the use of steam ships
meant the estuary at Topsham had become too shallow for larger
tonnage. Though John Holman had built a dry dock at Topsham in
1858, this was the only one and the firm later moved to London. The
last two ships to be built at Topsham were the *Haldon* and the
Exmouth, barges of 100 tons, in 1872-75.

Topsham museum also contains the waistcoat of Tom Putt (Curiosity
No 10).

Local Places of Interest
   28. A La Ronde, Exmouth
   77. Poltimore Fireplace in Church
Food and Accommodation
   Plenty available in Topsham

21 The Gateposts of Civilisation

Position: On the road from Hartland to Clovelly, not long before
Clovelly Dykes
Ordnance Map: Bude and Clovelly Sheet 190 1:50,000
Map Ref: SS 3025/2355
Access: The road from Hartland to Clovelly carries a lot of traffic, so
you may need to park some distance away and walk along the road.
The gateposts stand at the entrance to the field on the left-hand side of
the road a short distance before Providence Chapel.

Note: It is interesting to speculate what caused James Berryman,
landlord of the New Inn at Clovelly, to erect stone gateposts at the
entrance to a field on the edge of the road running from Hartland to
Clovelly. The left-hand post has a relief in metal of a woman's head in
Tudor dress engraved 'MARIE MARTR' with a shield; underneath
are verses
> 'Alpha thou art first I'm sure
> As Omega is in the West
> And thou'lt be first for evermore
> Now slumber on and rest
> This field was once a common moor
> Where gorse and rush grew free
> And now it grows green grass all o'er
> As all who pass may see'

This is dated January 10. A few months later, the other gatepost was
inscribed 'June 2 1902. King Edward VII crowned. Boer War ended. I
believe in church and state and all other religions that do good and to
be patriotic to my country . . . The above brings civilisation to our
great and mighty nation'.

Edward VII's reign must have seemed to many the dawn of a new
era. Towards the end of her exceptionally long reign (1837-1901),
Queen Victoria had become a recluse. The new king, by contrast, was
socially accomplished and keen to re-establish the pomp and ceremony
of majesty. Hence, he opened Parliament himself in February of that
year, something which the old queen had not done for 40 years. He also
encouraged imperialism by extending his regal title from 'of the United
Kingdom of Great Britain and Ireland' to include 'and of the British
Dominions beyond the Seas'. Beneath the surface, however, he was
much less hardworking than his mother and less intelligent.

The Boer War (1899-1902) was the climax of a long drawn-out
conflict. The ancestors of the Boers were those Dutch settlers who had
come to South Africa in the 17th century. In 1795, the British had

captured the Cape of Good Hope from the Dutch. Obliged to move by British expansion, the Dutch 'Voortrekkers' had established the independent states of Transvaal in 1852 and Orange Free State in 1854. The war began with the Battle of Mafeking when the British were besieged for 218 days.

The New Inn still exists in Clovelly, but opposite its former site; James Berryman was one of the last recorded owners, and may have been the person responsible for its relocation. In W. Walters's *Ilfracombe: A Guide to the North Devon Coast*, an advertisement for the New Inn, Clovelly, refers to the collection of antique china held by J. Berriman's (sic) wife.

Local Places of Interest
  50. Bucks Mills
Food and Accommodation
  Plenty available in Hartland and Clovelly

22 Gunrow Signal Station

Position: On Gunrow Down, between Hilsea Point and Stoke Point in the parish of Noss Mayo
Ordnance Map: Plymouth and Launceston Sheet 201 1:50,000
Map Ref: SX 5445/4595
Access: Drive from Noss Mayo through Revelstoke to Netton; turn right, continue along road until National Trust car-park on the left-hand side. Park the car, and continue by foot down the footpath towards the sea, crossing a stile, until you reach the Revelstoke carriage drive (a wide track). Turn left, and you will see Gunrow Signal Station perched on the slope above the carriage drive.

Note: Gunrow Signal Station was built in the late 18th century as a coastal look-out to check the enemy's movements. The earliest, and probably the most important of these signal stations was Maker Church Tower overlooking Plymouth Sound for which a set of signals dating from 1779 survives in the British Library in London.

The French revolutionary government had declared war on Britain in 1793, and by 1804 Napolean threatened invasion. In anticipation of his success, a medal was struck at Paris bearing the legend (inaccurately!) 'Frappé à Londres en 1804'. A force consisting of fishermen and others plying small boats had been established a few years earlier to man the coastline as the Sea Fencibles. Between 1805-14,

a telegraph system from London to Plymouth was operational. In the event, Bonaparte's hopes were never realized, but Gunrow, being in an ideal position for a look-out, was used again as an Observation post during World War Two. It is now in a dilapidated condition.

Local Places of Interest
40. Old Mother Hubbard's Cottage, Yealmpton
71. Toll-hut at Yealmbridge
Food and Accommodation
Plenty available in Newton Ferrers and Noss Mayo

23 Rajah Brooke of Sarawak

Position: In Sheepstor church
Ordnance Map: Torbay and South Dartmoor Sheet 202 1:50,000
Map Ref: SX 5600/6765

Note: The remote parish of Sheepstor on the south-western edge of
Dartmoor was the retirement home of Rajah James Brooke from 1863
until his death in 1868. Born the son of a judge in the East India
Company at Benares in 1803, Brooke was educated at Norwich, but
ran away from school. His early career was in the East India Company
until his resignation in 1830. In 1838, he travelled to Borneo and was
well received by the ruler of Sarawak, Rajah Muda Hassim, whose
nephew, the sultan of Brunei, ruled the whole island. Exploring the
country, he proved so helpful in putting down plots that he was
requested to accept the post of Rajah and instituted as such in 1841.
Here he stayed until retirement, laying down a code of law based on the
British, establishing a simple taxation scheme and attempting to
exterminate piracy. It is a tribute to his law-giving that Sarawak was
accepted as an independent state by America in 1850, and by the
United Kingdom in 1864, a year after he had left. His rule was not
universally popular, however; impugned for cruelty and illegal acts, he
was acquitted by a commission of inquiry at Singapore due to
insufficient evidence.

To help him in his work, he had money from Baroness Burdett
Coutts and moral support from his nephews, John Brooke and Charles
Anthoni Johnson, the sons of his sister Emma whom he made his
successors as Rajah. Charles Anthoni Johnson, later Brooke,
established a Civil Service in Sarawak and in 1888 the country was
accepted as a fully Independent State under the Protection of Great
Britain. Two of his three surviving sons, Charles Vyner and Bertram
also played their part in governing Sarawak. In 1946, it became a
British crown colony, and in 1963 part of the new state of Malaysia.

Rajah James Brooke lies buried in a large red Aberdeen granite
tomb in the Churchyard. There is a bust of him in the church.

Local Places of Interest
  38. Marchant's Cross, Meavy
  63. Drake's Leat, Clearbrook
  79. The Meavy Oak
Food and Accommodation
  The Royal Oak, Meavy

[42]

24 Lady Modyford's School

Position: In the centre of Buckland Monachorum village, on your left facing the church
Ordnance Map: Plymouth and Launceston Sheet 201 1:50,000
Map Ref: SX 4905/6840

Note: This school was endowed in March 1702 by Lady Elizabeth Modyford, the wealthy elderly widow of Sir James Modyford bart.

Under the terms of its establishment, Lady Modyford provided for the schoolmaster to receive £7/10/- (£7.50p) a year 'for teaching Children to read, write and cast accounts and for instructing them in the Church of England Catechism'. The six children were to be the offspring of parents too poor to pay for their education. A further £2/10/- (£2.50) a year was 'to be . . . laid out and bestowed in buying of each of the sd [said] 6 Scholars a bible with the Common Prayer &

liturgy of the Church of England in the same at the end of every 3 years (pupils were to remain at the school for 3 years) from Michaelmas then next & also a Coat and pair breeches of good strong blue woollen Cloth of about 2/8d (13p) or 3/- (15p) per yard with a towel or cravat for each of the sd [said] Six poor Scholars once in every 3 years time from Xmas then last'.

Much later, the schoolhouse fell into disrepair, and Manasseh Masseh Lopes repossessed it. Although he did not fulfil his intention to re-establish it, Sir Ralph Lopes of Maristow set it up again and arranged for its title to be clearly written in inch high letters over the facade 'Buckland School Repaired and Re-endowed by Sir Masseh Lopes 1830'.

Lady Modyford also arranged in her will of 1718-19 for the overseers of the poor in a number of parishes to give out a pennyworth of bread after Sunday morning service to poor parishioners not receiving parish relief. She died in 1724 at the age of 91.

Local Places of Interest
   38. Marchant's Cross, Meavy
   63. Drake's Leat, Clearbrook
   79. The Meavy Oak
Food and Accommodation
   Available in Buckland Monachorum and Yelverton

25 The Triumphal Arch, Filleigh

Position: Filleigh, west of South Molton
Ordnance Map: Barnstaple and Ilfracombe Sheet 180 1:50,000
Map Ref: SS 6680/2750
Access: Can be seen from the A361 running from South Molton to Barnstaple; the house is on your right-hand side, the arch at the top of the hill with an avenue of trees leading up to it on your left.

Note: The original home of the Fortescue family was at Wimpstone in Modbury, but a marriage to an heiress brought the family to North Devon. In 1719, Hugh Fortescue succeeded his father at the age of 24. Two years later, he inherited the Clinton title through his mother. Keen to build up the estate, he sold off land in South Devon, Somerset and Wiltshire, and set about acquiring as much land as he could near Filleigh. He pulled down the old house built by his grandfather in 1684, and erected Castle Hill on its site. Having travelled extensively in France and Italy like many young men of his generation, this was reflected in his choice of design: a formal French design with the vista from Castle Hill finishing on the skyline in the Triumphal Arch. From behind the Arch, the house could be seen with the mock castle on the hill behind. After Hugh's death in 1751, a less formal English design was adopted, though the Arch remained.

Hugo, fourth Earl Fortescue, writing in 1929 had this to say about his forebear. 'It may be conjectured that Lord Clinton was a conceited, self-important man. There are few country seats which force themselves so much on the view of passers-by as Castle Hill, and unless this had given him pleasure he could have made other arrangements. But though he built an imitation French château instead of a Georgian house and adorned the landscape, as was the fashion of the day, with a sham castle, a sham church at High Bray, and pseudo-classical temples, with the idea of making it more or less like a Claude Lorraine picture, he had sufficient taste and discrimination to acquire some good things abroad and to put some good plaster work and some good furniture into his new home'.

In May 1842, new plans were afoot. The then Lord Fortescue wrote to his 'dear Aunt El' in a letter, 'It would be a very great improvement if some road or other could be carried up to the Arch, and it would show the real shape of the ground and prevent that foreshortened effect which detracts so much from the beauty of the place at present'.

The Arch was rebuilt in 1961, having fallen down with the weight of the ivy. It was re-erected in memory of the fifth Earl and Countess by their family, friends and tenants.

Local Places of Interest
  43. Hugh Squier of South Molton
Food and Accommodation
  The Corn Dolly, South Molton is one of the best tea-shops in Devon

26 The Glazier's Agreement

Position: Brent Tor
Ordnance Map: Plymouth and Launceston Sheet 201 1:50,000
Map Ref: SX 4709/8045

Note: 'Brent Tarr. It's a Church on a very High hill, I believe nearest Heaven of any Church in England'. So wrote the distinguished Plymouth surgeon, Dr James Yonge, describing a journey he made in the spring of 1674. In fact, Brent Tor is 1,100 feet above sea level, and is clearly shown on a manuscript map of 1697 drawn from the high ground at Mount Edgcumbe by Edmund Dummer.

The word 'brant' probably means steep, and the choice of such a high spot, whilst appealing to the spirit, could prove daunting to the flesh. Richard Polwhele, in his early 19th century *History of Devonshire* noted that the parishioners of Brent Tor 'can never go to church

without the previous penance of climbing up this steep [rock], which they are so often obliged to attempt with the weariest industry, and in the lowliest attitude. In windy or rainy weather, the worthy pastor himself is frequently obliged to humble himself upon all fours, preparatory to his being exalted in the pulpit'.

Its exposed situation probably also meant higher repair bills. The churchwardens' accounts for the parish of Brentor note that on May 22 1781 it was agreed 'Between the Parrishoners of the Parrish of Brentorr at a meetting; and John Gloyne Glazour of Lamerton To keep and repair The Church Leads and Glass for one pound and one shilling per year as Long as he shall Live'. A note adds 'This Agreement Excepts all Axedents [accidents] such as Thunder and Lightenings Excepted by me John Gloyen'. A John Gloyne had acted as churchwarden, collecting the rates in 1779. However, the arrangement does not seem to have been very longlived. In 1781, Gloyne received £1/13/6 (£1.68p) 'for Repairing the Lids and glass'; in 1785, he took his guinea, but from 1790 onwards he had odd amounts of 10/6, (52p) 5/-, (25p) 5/2 (26p) in succeeding years.

The original church on this site was probably erected by Robert Giffard in the first half of the 12th century and given to Tavistock Abbey. The latter founded an annual fair here in 1232, spread over 3 days at Michaelmas, 28-30 September. At the Dissolution of the Monasteries, the church passed into the hands of the Duke of Bedford.

Local Places of Interest
  64. Wheal Betsy, Mary Tavy
Food and Accommodation
  Peter Tavy Inn (wholefood dishes)

27 The Magpie Squarson, Sabine Baring-Gould

Position: Lewtrenchard church
Ordnance Map: Plymouth and Launceston Sheet 201 1:50,000
Map Ref: SX 4571/8615

Note: Sabine Baring-Gould was that not uncommon product of self-confident Victorian England, a polymath. Born in Exeter in 1834, the eldest son of Edward Baring-Gould of Lewtrenchard, his first job was as a teacher, but at the age of 30 he was ordained deacon and a year later priest, eventually presenting himself to the family living at Lewtrenchard in 1881. He remained there until his death in 1924.

He was able to do this because since his father's death in 1872 he had also been Squire, hence he had a free hand to achieve whatever he wished without being frustrated. This may be the secret of his boundless energy. The motto on his tombstone, 'Paravi lucernam Christo Meo' (I have prepared a Lantern for my Christ') probably refers partly to his embellishment of Lewtrenchard church. His eclectic taste led him to install a 15th century brass chandelier from Belgium, a 15th century Flemish triptych and an eagle lectern from Brittany.

Sabine Baring-Gould's name will be familiar to many as the writer of 'Onward Christian Soldiers'; in fact, he wrote a multiplicity of books (159 between 1857-1920) on all sorts of subjects, not least local folklore and archaeology. Although he did much research, some of these works were lacking in the finer points of historical criticism. In some ways, he was ahead of his time in recording folksongs from Devon and Cornwall, whilst he also wrote local novels and was secretary of the Dartmoor exploration committee of the Devonshire Association, of which he was elected President in 1896. His many books were written by hand on a special desk later bequeathed to Exeter City Library.

One tale which must have intrigued Sabine is that of his ancestress, Madame Gould of Lewtrenchard or the White Lady. She died in 1795, but her tomb was opened by a hapless carpenter in 1832, whereupon she sat up, causing him to run off in fright. She followed him to his home, giving off so much light that he could see his own shadow before him. She had to be exorcized by seven clerics, who turned her into a white owl.

Sabine Baring-Gould and his wife Grace are buried in the churchyard. They had fourteen children.

Local Places of Interest
   29. Lydford Castle   73. Stowford Armour

28 A La Ronde

Position: Exmouth
Ordnance Map: Exeter, Sidmouth and surrounding area Sheet 192
1:50,000
Map Ref: SY 0050/8340
Access: A La Ronde lies just off a minor road linking the A376 (Exeter-Exmouth) to the B3180. Point-in-View is a bit farther down the road.

Note: A La Ronde house outside Exmouth was so called after the Basilica of San Vitale in Ravenna, an octagonal temple founded in the mid-6th century by Julian Argentario on the instructions of Bishop Ecclesius. The Basilica is one of the wonders of the world because its architectural style is so original and its decoration, particularly the mosaics, so rich.

A La Ronde was built by Miss Jane Parminter, born in 1750 of a Huguenot merchant family established in Barnstaple. Miss Parminter was a great traveller, which no doubt explains her choice of a house. At the age of 23, she had taken over responsibility for a young cousin, Mary Parminter, and over twenty years later in 1795 they bought the land on which A La Ronde was to be built. They lived here together until Jane's death at the age of 61 in 1811.

East of A La Ronde is the chapel Point-in-View with the neighbouring school and almshouses built in 1811. Point-in-View, where Jane Parminter was buried, was a Dissenting Chapel, part of whose purpose was to promote Christianity among Jews: 'Some Points in View We All Pursue'. The almshouses were built to house 4 spinsters over 50 years of age, one of whom would teach six pauper girls. Should any of the applicants be Jews who had converted to Christianity, positive discrimination should be exercised in their favour. Every year on 6 November, the anniversary of Jane Parminter's death, each of the little girls was to receive 'a stuff gown, a straw bonnet, a linen cap and a Vandyke tippet'.

Jane Parminter also provided in her will that the oak trees on her estate at A La Ronde 'shall remain standing and the hand of man shall not be raised against them, till Israel returns and is restored to the land of Promise'.

Local Places of Interest
   19. Joan Raleigh's Tomb, East Budleigh
Food and Accommodation
   Available in East Budleigh

29 Lydford Castle

Position: Lydford
Ordnance Map: Plymouth and Launceston Sheet 201 1:50,000
Map Ref: SX 5080/8480

Note: The Pipe Roll accounts (so called because when rolled up they are the shape of a pipe) kept at the Public Record Office in London reveal that Lydford Castle was built at Michaelmas 1195. (Michaelmas Day is September 29: the Feast of St Michael and All Angels). It cost £74, of which £32 was provided out of income from Devon lands, and the rest out of moneys from the stannary or tin revenue in Cornwall. It was intended 'for the custody of the king's prisoners': in other words, to deal with those who contravened the stannary laws.

The stannary laws arose out of the special right of people working precious metals to sue and be sued before the Vice-Warden of the

Stannaries (though this did not apply in cases involving life, limb or land). The office of Warden of the Stannaries was instituted in 1198, soon after the building of the Castle. The Warden's job was to summon the 96 representatives of the stannaries together at Crockern Tor on Dartmoor. Surviving statutes show that the stannary courts met here from 1494-1730. The court of the Lord Warden was finally merged in the Court of Appeal in 1873, though the Vice-Warden's court survived until 1896.

In 1512, Richard Strode, Member of Parliament for Plympton, was convicted in the stannary courts for having promoted a bill to lessen tinning activities near ports because these were silting up the harbours. Although imprisoned in the Castle, he did not suffer the fate described by the poet William Browne: 'I have often heard of Lydford law/ How in the morn they hang and draw.'

The castle is square, built of stone and had two storeys. It superseded an early Norman motte and wooden bailey, the remains of which are still apparent. The Pipe Roll accounts show it being stocked with food and provisions in case of siege soon after it was built: 15 flanks of bacon, 10 cows, 10 loads of rye, 20 quarters of oats, a ton of wine and other necessaries.

Lydford had been important since the reign of Alfred the Great (the late 9th century) when it formed part of a chain of national defence; a century later, it effectively thwarted the Danish invaders in 997. From the reign of Ethelred II beginning in 979 until that of Edward the Confessor ending in 1066, its mint issued silver pennies. Lydford was also important in the Middle Ages because the whole of the royal forest of Dartmoor lay within the parish.

Local Places of Interest
27. The Magpie Squarson: Sabine Baring-Gould of Lewtrenchard
Food and Accommodation
The Castle Inn, Lydford and other hotels there

The Bridge, Bideford

30 Bideford's Medieval Long Bridge

Position: Bideford
Ordnance Map: Barnstaple and Ilfracombe Sheet 180 1:50,000
Map Ref: SX 4545/2650

Note: The earliest bridge over the River Torridge at Bideford was made of wood, probably built by Sir Theobald Grenville in the 14th century. Later, a stone bridge was erected around and above it. The oldest parts of the present bridge were built in the 16th century, but it has been much repaired due to constant use over the centuries.

The bridge consists of 24 arches which vary in size and in shape. One theory as to why this is so is that parishes nearby donated the arches, hence a large arch (some spans are as wide as 25 foot) denotes a wealthy parish, a smaller arch (some are as narrow as 12 foot) one less wealthy. Certainly, the style of the arches reflects their origins: pointed or Gothic arches (like seals) suggest an ecclesiastical builder, whilst the later semi-circular arches are more likely to have been built by the civic authorities.

The bridge is shown on the earliest borough seal of the 14th century, and again on a seal appended to a deed of 1474 where it has a chapel at either end. It was unique in having two chapels; the chapel at the east end was named after St Anne, that at the west end after All Saints. Though apparently neither of these was endowed, a third chapel was built 'for the use of the fraternity of the Blessed Virgin Mary . . . for the upkeep, repair and maintenance of the said bridge'. In return for donating land to the fraternity, a man might gain a share in all the prayers and masses held there for the benefit of his soul and the souls of those dear to him.

Over the centuries, the bridge amassed considerable wealth, hence the maps of the bridge lands drawn in 1745. Two hundred years later, it had acquired a total of fifty-one properties, considerably more than was needed for its upkeep, so the additional money was spent on charitable projects such as Bideford grammar school.

Bridgeland Street betrays its origin by its name. It was laid out about 1690 by Nathaniel Gascoyne.

Local Places of Interest
16. Medieval Wall-Painting, Weare Giffard
76. Tawstock Gatehouse
Food and Accommodation
Plenty available in Bideford. The Waterfront Restaurant, Appledore

31 Childe's Tomb

Position: Dartmoor, SE of Princetown
Ordnance Map: Torbay and South Dartmoor Sheet 202 1:50,000
Map Ref: SX 6260/7030
Access: From the centre of Princetown, take the minor road to Tor
Royal. Continue until the road stops. Park car, and continue on foot,
skirting Fox Tor Mire to Childe's Tomb which lies SE of the road.

Note: Legend has it that a landed Plymstock man called Childe was out
hunting on Dartmoor when he lost his way and the rest of the hunt.
Bitterly cold, the best way he could think of to save himself was to kill
and skin his horse and take refuge in the carcass. However, he died of
exposure despite these precautions.

Childe had no children, and there was competition to bury him
because, under the terms of his will, his lands would belong to the
church where he was buried. The parishioners of Plymstock, hearing
that Tavistock people planned to bury him in the Abbey Church,
gathered at the Tavy bridge in order to intercept them. Tavistock
outwitted them, however, by quickly constructing a little bridge
elsewhere to cross the river. This new bridge was called Guilebridge
because it had been built by guile; this has now been corrupted to Guild
Bridge because it goes to Tavistock Guildhall.

Several details of this folk-story do not add up. According to
Tristram Risdon, Childe's tomb was inscribed 'They fyrste that fynde
and brings mee to my grave, The priorie of Plymstoke they shall have',
but there is no evidence that a priory existed at Plymstock. Likewise, it
is a considerable distance from the site of Childe's Tomb near
Princetown to Tavistock Abbey. A grain of truth may lie in the fact that
Tavistock Abbey had possessed the manor of Plymstock since the
Domesday Book, thus suggesting that the events of this tale took place
before then.

Local Places of Interest
    2. Powdermills, Postbridge
  61. Dartmoor letter-box, Ducks' Pool
Food and Accommodation
    Available in Princetown

32 Colyton Octagonal Lantern

Position: On Colyton Church Tower
Ordnance Map: Exeter, Sidmouth and surrounding area Sheet 192
1:50,000
Map Ref: SY 2460/9410

Note: Colyton church's octagonal lantern was built in the 15th century
on top of the existing Norman tower and was intended as a navigational
light for boats approaching Colyton haven. Such lanterns are rare, but
others exist in the east of the country: Ely Cathedral, Boston in

Lincolnshire and Fotheringay in Rutland. At that date, the mouth of the River Axe formed a broad estuary up which craft could sail. In 1513, Colyton port gave ships for Henry VIII's war against France, whilst in 1575-83 money was gathered in local churches to make good damage to the harbour.

Harbours needed constant attention. The combined effects of storms (a bad one in 1377 wrecked Lyme Regis nearby) and the sea eroding the eastern headland meant a bank of shingle had built up at the estuary mouth in the fifteenth century, preventing all but small boats from travelling upwater. Bishop Lacy made some attempt to remedy the situation in 1450 by granting an indulgence of 40 days to anyone who would contribute financially towards making good the harbour.

The portrait of Chaucer's skipper from Dartmouth in the prologue to *The Canterbury Tales* describes the knowledge gleaned from experience of a navigator in the late 14th century, a generation or two before the lantern was built

> 'As for his skill in reckoning his tides,
> Currents and many other risk besides
> Moons, harbours, pilots, he had such dispatch
> That none from Hull to Carthage was his match . . .
> And he knew all the havens as they were
> From Gottland to the Cape of Finisterre . . .'

Colyton in the early 16th century was the fourth wealthiest town in Devon: twelve men, including merchants and farmers, were valued at £660 in the tax assessment of 1523.

The building by the entrance gates of the churchyard once housed Colyton grammar-school (established in 1546).

Local Places of Interest
　12. Loughwood Meeting-House, Dalwood
　49. Axminster Carpet Factory
　53. Shute Gatehouse
Food and Accommodation
　Plenty in Axminster

33 Albemarle Villas

Position: Stoke Damerel
Ordnance Map: Plymouth and Launceston Sheet 201 1:50,000
Map Ref: SX 4585/5495
Access: Take Milehouse Road from the crossroads at Central Park.
This changes half-way down into Devonport Road. Albemarle Villas is
the last turning but one on the left-hand side before Devonport Road
merges with Paradise Road into Fore Street.

Note: Albemarle Villas is a group of eight houses in classical style built
by John Foulston (1772-1842) between 1820-27. Foulston had come to
Plymouth from London on winning a competition to build the Royal
Hotel, Assembly Rooms and Theatre in 1811. Although the Theatre
complex no longer survives, several of his other buildings, both public
and private, do because for a number of years in the early 19th century
he was Plymouth's most fashionable architect and was thus an ideal
choice to design these pleasant houses for the well-to-do in the newly
arising suburb of Stoke. No house is exactly the same as its neighbour,
though each has a verandah or balcony. One of the villas, however, No
3, was bombed during World War Two and had to be rebuilt.
Apparently, the two ladies then living in it had gone to stay at
Yelverton when firebombs were dropped on Albemarle Villas. Owners
of the other houses extinguished the fires, but No 3 was left burning by
default.

Foulston worked in each of the three towns of Plymouth, Devonport
and Stonehouse (they were not combined into the modern city of
Plymouth until 1914). He was the architect of Union Street built 1812-
20 connecting George Street in Plymouth with Stonehouse; the
Octagon was intended as a centre-point in the street.

Foulston's influence architecturally at this date must have been
prodigious, as reflected in this ditty:

> 'Augustus of Rome was for building renowned
> And of marble he left what of brick he had found:
> But was not our Foulston a very great master?
> He found us all brick and left us all plaster'.

A set of 23 watercolours by Foulston of his designs survives in
Plymouth City Museum and Art Gallery.

Local Places of Interest
  34. Devonport Column
  65. Monument to Aggie Weston, Weston Mill cemetery

34 Devonport Column

Position: Ker Street, Devonport
Ordnance Map: Plymouth and Launceston Sheet 201 1:50,000
Map Ref: SX 4530/5440

Note: The building of Plymouth Dock from 1689 onwards gave rise to a new town just beyond it, which grew incredibly fast as a result of the wars in the eighteenth century. By 1815, this new town of Dock had some 32,000 inhabitants compared with Plymouth's 22,000 and it was indignant at being regarded as 'a mere offshoot of the borough of Plymouth'. So on 1 January 1824 it was granted permission to change its name to Devonport, and this column erected to John Foulston's design to commemorate the event.

The Column is made of granite quarried near the River Tamar, and rises 124 feet above the street below. A remarkable feature is that each stone was hoisted and set without the use of scaffolding. The Column can be ascended by climbing a spiral staircase within the shaft which gives onto a gallery at the top. However, the staircase is kept locked and the key held by Plymouth City Council.

Unfortunately, all did not go quite according to plan in erecting the Column. A contemporary noted 'The Foundation Stone was laid on the 12 of August 1824, and it was originally proposed to place a colossal statue of His Majesty on the summit but certain individuals having refused to answer the engagements to which they had affixed their names as subscribers, the parties employed in the erection have not been paid; and there is, consequently, very little chance of its being completed in the manner originally contemplated. Instead of being a trophy, recording the honours which belong to a high sounding name, it is likely to remain a memorial of the neglect and injustice with which the indigent widow of the builder, and others have been treated, to whom considerable sums are now due.'

Foulston was an advocate of mixing architectural styles. Near the base of the Column can be found the classical Devonport Town Hall (modelled on the Parthenon) and the Civil and Military Library built in the Egyptian style.

Local Places of Interest
33. Albemarle Villas, Devonport
65. Monument to Aggie Weston, Weston Mill cemetery
Food and Accommodation
Plenty in Plymouth

[60]

[61]

35 The Punctual Miller, Matthew the Miller Clock

Position: St Mary Steps church, Exeter
Ordnance Map: Exeter, Sidmouth and surrounding area Sheet 192
1:50,000
Map Ref: SX 9175/9228

Note: Matthew is represented by the man seated above the dial. In real life, he was a wealthy miller, so punctual in his hours of passing between the city and his house at Cricklepit that neighbours could tell the time of day by his movements.

The clock was erected in 1619-21 by two successive churchwardens, James Taylor and Matthew Symons. Unfortunately, they quarrelled later, Symons arguing that he had borne the full charge. However, when the case came up in court, it was established that it was Taylor who had set up the clock and dial in 1619 whilst Symons 'did only sett up the two Jacks wch [which] play at every qr [quarter] of an howre [hour] and another statue of tymber called Mathew the Miller sitting in his chaire wch playeth out at every howers [hour's] end, and also the two quarter bells under the feete of the sd [said] two Jacks and the name of the sd Mathew Symons in full letters and the yeare of our Lord (1621) guilted [gilded] with gould [gold], with a loader horse and baggs uppon him and a loder uppon that carved in Free stone and the portrayture of the Mill house and of ye trees'. The packhorse and trees are now gone, and the statue of Matthew was replaced by a replica in 1980. The jacks, who sit on either side of Matthew, probably represent his sons.

The maker of the clock was another Matthew, Matthew Hoppin.

Local Places of Interest
   36. Medieval Aqueducts, Exeter
   46. Exeter Catecombs
   56. Plaque to Matthew Godwin, Exeter Cathedral
Food and Accommodation
   Plenty in Exeter. Cooling's Wine Bar, Gandy Street

36 Exeter's Medieval Aqueducts

Position: Exeter
Ordnance Map: Exeter, Sidmouth and surrounding area Sheet 192
1:50,000
Map Ref: SX 9230/9285

Note: Exeter's underground passages may have been originally constructed by the Romans to supply water to the Baths.

Supposition apart, however, the passages are referred to in a deed of 1226 indicating their use for bringing water from St Sidwell's well to St Nicholas Priory. The Priory was allowed one third of the water by the Dean and Chapter of Exeter Cathedral.

In 1346 the Cathedral Fabric Rolls show the accounts for paying workmen to dig out the conduit or aqueduct; they received sums varying from 8d (3p) to 10d a week, whilst 'R the plumber' had 16d (7p) for preparing 5 lead pipes. However, in 1420 the civic dignitaries made up their minds to become independent of the cathedral authorities, and bring an independent supply of water from a well near that supplying the Dean and Chapter. In 1436 a new conduit was built, which remained in use until 1770.

Local Places of Interest
    35. The Punctual Miller: Matthew the Miller Clock, Exeter
    46. Exeter Catecombs
    56. Plaque to Matthew Godwin, Exeter Cathedral
Food and Accommodation
    Plenty in Exeter

37 Seating in Hartland church

Position: Hartland church
Ordnance Map: Bude and Clovelly Sheet 190 1:50,000
Map Ref: SS 2350/2475

Note: In earlier centuries when nearly all the parish attended church, the position where a person sat reflected his or her social standing. Disputes over this matter were sometimes acrimonious.

In Hartland church, Hugh Prust of Thorney 'did at his owne charges paie for the erectinge of all the seats pews and seages' [the French word for chair is 'siege'] in St Mary's Guild in the North Chancel aisle. One pew just below the right-hand side of the rood-screen has a bench-end with 'HUWE PRIST' carved on it and a scroll design.

A later Hugh Prust figures prominently on a seating plan for Hartland Church of 1613, which records in detail who was to sit where. Hugh Prust has seat No 1 in the South aisle. The preamble to the plan notes 'we . . . have fixed on every seate, the parties names therein expressed to sit, and have publiquely and solemnly pronounced in the said parish church of Hartland after dyvine service ended on the next Saboth day after our agreement and subscription hereunto'. Not quite everybody had a named place, however; part of the aisle to the north of the chancel was to hold 'such sufficient young married men as are not seated in the life of their parents paying each of them iis for ye same and to be placed by the churchwardens for ye tyme being'.

The seating plan is kept in a room over the north porch, known as the Pope's Chamber. It would probably have housed the sacristan, living there to watch over the precious objects belonging to the church. In the latter half of the sixteenth century, some churches also kept the parish armour there. Since the reign of Edward II, each parish had been required to provide one or more soldiers equipped for war at home or abroad.

Local Places of Interest
21. The Gateposts of Civilisation
Food and Accommodation
Hartland and Clovelly; Anchor Inn, Hartland

38 Marchant's Cross, Meavy

Position: Meavy
Ordnance Map: Plymouth and Launceston Sheet 201 1:50,000
Map Ref: SX 5460/6680
Access: Drive through Meavy village, past the church and public house. Take the road on your right. Marchant's Cross is opposite a farm just near the bridge.

Note: Marchant's Cross may have been so called because it was erected by a particular merchant or guild of merchants. Standing over eight foot high, it lies on the Abbots' Way running from Buckfast Abbey to Tavistock and Buckland Abbeys. It would also have been useful for anyone making the journey from the churches of Meavy and Sampford Spiney to their parent foundation at Plympton Priory.

Until just over forty years ago, Marchant's Cross was believed to be the Smalacumbacrosse mentioned in a charter of 1291 by Isabella de Fortibus. However, close examination of the boundaries mentioned in the charter made it clear that this was not the case.

In the mid-19th century, the cross was believed to mark the grave of a suicide, and it was thought that travellers intending to cross the moor would say their prayers for a safe passage in front of it.

Local Places of Interest
   23. Rajah Brooke of Sarawak
   63. Drake's Leat, Clearbrook
   79. The Meavy Oak
Local Places of Interest
   The Roval Oak, Meavy; Yelverton

39 Adrian Swete's conduit, Modbury

Position: Top of the hill in Brownston Street, Modbury
Ordnance Map: Torbay and South Dartmoor Sheet 202 1:50,000
Map Ref: SX 6590/5180

Note: This conduit in Brownston Street for the supply of fresh water to Modbury was built by Adrian Swete of Traine, the finest house near the town. This is the best example of the four that were built and is the one used to convey the main supply of water. Two others were given by Nicholas Trist as lord of the manor in 1708 and placed in Church Street and Galpin Street. Originally, these conduits would have stood in the centre of the street. The one above was moved to the side when Traine House was built, because it spoilt the view. The others were probably moved when a new road was built. They are all made of granite moorstone.

The Swete family had lived at Traine since the reign of Henry VIII and were benefactors to the town. In 1684, John Swete donated land at the top of Galpin Street on which almshouses were later built. Adrian Swete, the donor of the conduit, left £40 in his will to buy a silver flagon for the church.

Local Places of Interest
 40. Old Mother Hubbard's Cottage, Yealmpton
 71. Toll-hut at Yealmbridge
Food and Accommodation
 Exeter Inn; Modbury Pippin (both at Modbury)

40 Old Mother Hubbard's Cottage

Position: Yealmpton
Ordnance Map: Torbay and South Dartmoor Sheet 202 1:50,000
Map Ref: SX 5810/5180
Access: On the A379 from Plymouth to Modbury, right-hand side towards the end of the village.

Note: The Mother Hubbard rhymes were written by Sarah Catherine Martin, daughter of Sir Henry Martin, Resident Commissioner of the Navy at Portsmouth, when she was staying at the house of her brother-in-law, John Pollexfen Bastard of Kitley House. She also drew the pictures for the original version, which was published in 1804. The character of Mother Hubbard was based on the housekeeper at Kitley, who retired to the cottage above.

Some twenty years before in 1785, the then Prince William Henry (later William IV) had fallen in love with Sarah and proposed marriage. A lieutenant on board *HMS Hebe*, he often visited her family home. Sarah discreetly declined, however, and her behaviour was considered most proper by all those involved. She never married.

A first edition of the Mother Hubbard rhymes was for many years in the hands of the Bastard family of Kitley.

Local Places of Interest
    39. Adrian Swete's Conduit, Modbury
    71. Toll-hut at Yealmbridge
Food and Accommodation
    Available at Yealmpton and Modbury

41 Moretonhampstead Almshouses

Position: At the eastern end of the town, on the left-hand side of the
B3212 to Dunsford
Ordnance Map: Okehampton and North Dartmoor Sheet 191 1:50,000
Map Ref: SX 7540/8605

Note: The present building on this site, Moretonhampstead
almshouses, was built in 1637, but replaced an earlier almshouse –
Moreton's Medieval Hospital. The latter was probably the first
building dedicated to such a purpose in Devon and was established in
about 1450.

The origin of almshouses lies in the provision for hospitality to
strangers and almsgiving in monasteries. Later, almshouses were often
founded as private charities and particularly intended for sick and
elderly people. The Poor Law of 1601, which was to be operational for
more than 200 years, had provided for the churchwardens and
overseers of the parish to set the able-bodied poor to work and collect
rates to administer the system from other parishioners. Many people,
however, would have fallen outside this provision.

Our word 'almoner' derives from this same tradition of helping those
who may not be in a position to help themselves. One of the best
surviving examples of such an almshouse is the Hospice de Beaune,
near Dijon in France, the interior of which can be visited. Beaune is
where some of the finest Burgundy wines are grown, and until recently,
the profits from selling the wine at auction on the third Sunday in
November were devoted to the Hospice. The Hospice de Beaune was
founded in 1443, just a few years before Moreton's Medieval Hospital.

By 1938 the almshouses were condemned as unfit to be inhabited but were bought on behalf of the town and later acquired by the National Trust.

Local Places of Interest
    70. Jay's Grave, Manaton
Food and Accommodation
    Mearsdon Manor, Moretonhampstead; the Ring of Bells, North Bovey

The Copstone, Copplestone

42 The Copstone

Position: Copplestone
Ordnance Map: Okehampton and North Dartmoor Sheet 191 1:50,000
Map Ref: SS 7760/0250
Access: In the centre of the road at the intersection of the A3072 with the road from Newbuildings.

Note: The Copstone is very ancient. At one time, it stood on the meeting point of routes from Crediton, Barnstaple, Okehampton and Morchard Bishop. Already by the Charter of King Edgar (king of England 959-75) granting 3 hides of land to his thegn Aelfhere in 974, it was well-known, and an endorsement on the back of the charter runs 'If anyone therefore shall take it away from the aforesaid place, or in any wise diminish it, may he, stricken with a perpetual curse, perish everlastingly with the Devil; unless he strive by due reparation to make atonement'.

However, on 13 March 1969 it was moved by Devon County Council. They thought it a nuisance to drivers, so they moved it ten yards north-west and gave it a stone plinth. It had been put on a plinth about 1850.

The stone probably originally formed part of a cross, since it has a mortice hole in which another stone could be fixed. Though much weathered, it is possible to make out scrollwork patterns on the shafts. This interlacing is very unusual for a stone found on the east side of the River Tamar, although in northern England, particularly Northumbria, it is quite common. The name 'Copplestone' probably derives from 'cop' meaning 'head', hence headstone. It is quite possible that it was erected by the bishops of Devonshire, part of whose estate lies in the parish of Crediton, so that their serfs and churls could say their prayers here since it is a considerable distance from any church.

The Copplestone family may have drawn their name from this cross. A rhyme to illustrate the family's ancient roots runs
'Crocker, Cruwys, and Copplestone,
When the Conqueror came, were found at home'

Local Places of Interest
  1. The Dowrich Ghost, Sandford
  74. Sandford School
Food and Accommodation
  Available in Crediton

43 In Praise of Arithmetic: Hugh Squier of South Molton

Position: On facade of South Molton Town Hall
Ordnance Map: Barnstaple and Ilfracombe Sheet 180 1:50,000
Map Ref: SS 7135/2585

Note: South Molton Town Hall (1740-43) bears the bust of Hugh Squier of Townhouse, who built and endowed the grammar-school there.

Hugh is believed to have moved to London, where he became a merchant. Sadly, although he married and had four children, none survived to maturity so in 1682 he set out his instructions for his new foundation. Children hoping to attend were expected to have a reading knowledge of the Book of Psalms since 'this Schooll shall be chiefly to teach good writing and Arithmetick.

'Arithmetic, as necessary as our dayly bread, or salt unto our meat, ye thing wch [which] every man is making use of, every houre of all his life, if that he bee awake – for want whereof, some persons who are poor, mistake, in thinking they are rich, and others who are Rich, mistake, and think that they are poor. What better knouelledge [knowledge] than for a man to Know himself, wh [which] can not be done in any tollerable measure wth out [without] this art, so necessary both by sea and land, no man can go to sea wth out it, and at land, that man will badly thrive who can't make up a reckoning of wt [what] hee doth nothing more necessary to every ones prosperity than to be able (to) use his pen'.

This preference for practical knowledge over traditional school subjects such as grammar and the Classics was often associated with religious Dissent. Mathematics would have been useful both for the art of navigation and surveying.

Local Places of Interest
  25. The Triumphal Arch, Filleigh
  76. Tawstock Gatehouse
Food and Accommodation
  The Corn Dolly, South Molton is one of the best tea-shops in Devon!

44 The Ten Commandments Stone

Position: Buckland Beacon
Ordnance Map: Okehampton and North Dartmoor Sheet 191 1:50,000
Map Ref: SX 7350/7310
Access: From Buckland-in-the-Moor, take the minor road to Ausewell
Cross, where you turn left. Buckland Beacon lies about half-way along,
on the left-hand side of the road. Park car beyond, where the road
enters open moorland, and follow track. The Ten Commandments
stones are just below the summit of the beacon near your approach.

Note: 'It hath been the wisdom of the Church of England, ever since
the first compiling of her Publick Liturgy, to keep the mean between
the two extremes, of too much stiffness in refusing, and of too much
easiness in admitting any variation from it'. The golden mean of
Anglicanism was established soon after the break with the Roman
Catholic church, and has been a fundamental trait ever since,
contributing towards its survival. As we have seen (Curiosity No 18),
beneath a reserved exterior, passions can run deep about the relative
merits of different forms of worship.

  Since before the Great War (1914-18), attempts had been made to
prepare a new Book of Common Prayer giving more credence to
Anglo-Catholic practices. However, although the House of Lords
accepted the revised version, the House of Commons rejected it twice

in 1928. Their decision was popular with many of the laity, but many clergy liked the new version. In the event, the House of Convocation (a provincial synod, called to deliberate on church matters) illegally permitted bishops to use the new Prayer Book 'during the present emergency' and, since this has never been revoked, its illegal use has continued.

However, Mr William Whitley, owner of Buckland Court and lord of the manor, was so delighted with the House of Commons's rejection of the new Prayer Book that he employed a sculptor, W.A. Clement, to engrave the Ten Commandments on tablets of stone on Buckland Beacon. The tablets have weathered over the years, and it is hard to read the engraving on one of them.

Mr Clement of Exeter lived in a hut near the site and was inevitably known as Moses.

Local Places of Interest
   66. My Dear Mother Clock, Buckland church
Food and Accommodation
   Available in Ashburton

45 Gatehouse to Cornworthy Priory

Position: Cornworthy
Ordnance Map: Torbay and South Dartmoor Sheet 202 1:50,000
Map Ref: SX 8235/5560
Access: From Cornworthy church, take the road to Furzehill Cross, turn right to go down Water Lane and take the second turning left. The gatehouse is near the edge of a field and is clearly visible from the road.

Note: The gatehouse is all that remains of the Augustinian priory of nuns at Cornworthy. Founded between 1231-38 (though the gatehouse is not recorded until 40 years later), Cornworthy was the smallest of the three Devon convents, having only about seven inhabitants.

Though the nuns were supposed, according to their Rule, to work themselves, we know that in 1521 Bishop Vesey of Exeter (who had overall responsibility for nunneries in the diocese) reprimanded them for keeping too many servants! They were also in trouble for sleeping in separate cells instead of a single dormitory, for eating on their own instead of in common, and for not saying their Divine Office together. Slackness may have crept in during the time of Prioress Thomasyn Dynham, who ruled from c1470-1520.

Cornworthy was not alone in these transgressions. In many nunneries, chatting after Compline, the last service of the day, meant nuns found it hard to rise at the appointed hour next morning, or, if they did, they might snooze during the first Office or gabble their words. Gabbling was so common that there was supposed to be a little devil called Tittivillus who gathered up all the missed syllables into a sack and took them to the Devil: if he did not collect a thousand pokes full, he would be beaten!

Cornworthy Priory was dissolved in 1537 when the Prioress was given a pension of 13/- (65p) a year and the land and buildings passed into secular hands.

Local Places of Interest
    7. Daymark, Dartmouth Harbour
    67. Galmpton Warborough Windmill
Food and Accommodation
    Available in Dartmouth and Totnes

46 The Exeter Catacombs

Position: Exeter
Ordnance Map: Exeter, Sidmouth and surrounding area Sheet 192
1:50,000
Map Ref: SX 6195/9255
Access: From the Royal Albert Museum in Queen Street, Exeter, walk
down Northernhay Street, cross the road and go up Bartholomew
Street East. The catacombs are in the disused cemetery (now a park)
beneath you and can be reached by walking down some steps.

Note: The catacombs, known as the Lower Cemetery, were
consecrated on 24 August 1837, exactly 200 years after the land had
first been devoted to this use as St Bartholomew's Burial Ground (24
August is St Bartholomew's Day). After September 1837, people could
only be buried in the vaults. The catacombs themselves were
constructed out of volcanic stone erected on the former city wall and a
series of arches.
    Because the catacombs were designed for use both by Anglicans and
Dissenters, two entrances and two toolhouses were built. The western
entrance was intended for Anglicans, the eastern for Dissenters,
although in fact very few people were buried in the Anglican section
and probably none in that of the Dissenters. It seems that the syndicate
which had been formed to run the cemetery went bankrupt.

Local Places of Interest
    35. The Punctual Miller: Matthew the Miller Clock, Exeter
    46. Exeter Catacombs
    56. Plaque to Matthew Godwin, Exeter Cathedral
Food and Accommodation
    Plenty in Exeter. Cooling's Wine Bar, Gandy Street

*A drawing of the whistling
cock weather-vane, Ottery St
Mary*

47 Chanticleer: The Whistling Cock

Position: On Ottery St Mary church tower
Ordnance Map: Exeter, Sidmouth and surrounding area Sheet 192
1:50,000
Map Ref: SY 0985/9555

Note: The whistling cock weather-vane on the church tower at Ottery
St Mary may be the oldest still in use in this country. Like the clock in
the South transept of the church, and the wooden eagle lantern painted
in gold, it was probably installed by Bishop John de Grandisson of
Exeter in the early 14th century. Bishop Grandisson had lofty
aspirations for the church which he saw as an embryonic version of
Exeter Cathedral.

Cocks on church towers have a special significance, harking back to
pagan times, when cocks were placed on top of temples to ward off evil
spirits. The cock at Ottery St Mary has two trumpet-like tubes running
from its breast to its tail, which used to cause a whistling noise in strong
winds, but are now corroded.

Symbolically the cock represents both repentance and vigilance.
Hugo de Sancto Victore wrote in his *Mystical Mirrour of the Church*
that 'the cock in the deep watches of the night divideth the hours
thereof with his song, and arouseth the sleepers. He foretelleth the
approach of day, but first he stirreth up himself to crow by the striking
of his wings . . .' In the early Middle Ages, the length of an hour
varied according to the seasons, a daylight hour in summer being
considerably longer than in winter, due to the duration of daylight.
Regular hours were a consequence of the introduction of clocks.
Bishop Grandisson's clock is first referred to among college account
rolls of 1437-38.

Local Places of Interest
   10. Tom Putt's Beech Avenue, Gittisham
   48. Thorn Tree, Salcombe Regis
Food and Accommodation
   King's Arms Hotel. Plenty of up-market eating places

48 Thorn Tree

Position: Salcombe Regis
Ordnance Map: Exeter, Sidmouth and surrounding area Sheet 192
1:50,000
Map Ref: SY 1485/8910
Access: Take the A3052 running from Newton Poppleford to Colyford;
turn off right towards Salcombe Regis; take right-hand fork up the hill;
the Thorn Tree is at the next fork just before the road forks again for
Salcombe Regis.

Note: Because the hawthorn is a thorny shrub, or small tree, it is often
used for growing hedges and hence as a boundary. The granite pillar
and notice erected in 1939 on the site of the present Thorn Tree tells us
that the tree here marked the boundary between the cultivated land of
the valley and the common field of the hill. Thorn Farm nearby, where

a manor court was probably once held, derives its name from this tree.

Tradition has it that there has been a thorn tree at Salcombe Regis since Saxon times. It was intimately connected with the surrounding community: local people believed that it reflected the life of the parish, so when it died, a new one was soon planted. An earlier Thorn Tree may have stood in the churchyard, quite some distance from this site.

Local Places of Interest
32. Colyton Octagonal Lantern
47. The Whistling Cock, Ottery St Mary
Food and Accommodation
Available in Sidmouth or Seaton

49 The 18th Century Carpet Factory, Axminster

Position: North-east of the church
Ordnance Map: Taunton and Lyme Regis Sheet 193 1:50,000
Map Ref: SY 2985/9865

Note: In 1754 Thomas Whitty, a cloth-weaver from Axminster, saw 'one of the best and largest Turkey carpets in England' when visiting a London ironmonger. He was so impressed that, although unsure precisely how the carpet had been made, he tried experimenting on a day when the factory was empty because his workers were enjoying the Fair, 25 April 1755. Soon after, Thomas had an opportunity of studying the new techniques in more detail at Mr Parisot's factory in Fulham. By midsummer 1755, his children were at work on the new carpets, and orders were coming in.

   Thomas Whitty's original carpet factory and house still stand in Axminster, to the north-east of the church. A piece of hand-knotted carpet produced by Thomas Whitty is still kept in Axminster church, with its original colour intact because vegetable dyes were used. When the Axminster carpets were first made, each was such hard work that a peal of bells was rung, and the carpet carried in procession to be blessed before its use! In 1835, carpet-making was moved to Wilton outside Salisbury but it was re-established in Axminster in 1936.

Local Places of Interest
   12. Loughwood Meeting House
   32. Colyton Octagonal Lantern
   53. Shute Gatehouse
Food and Accommodation
   Available in Axminster

50 Bucks Mills

Position: On the left-hand side of the A39 running from Clovelly Dykes
to Bideford
Ordnance Map: Bude and Clovelly Sheet 190 1:50,000
Map Ref: SS 3555/2365

Note: Limekilns are frequently to be found along the estuaries and
creeks of Devon, but the square limekiln at Bucks Mills is exceptional
in view of its size and dramatic position overlooking Bideford Bay.

Erected in 1760 by Robert Davey, it must have required a
considerable outlay of capital, though eventually such kilns often
showed a respectable profit. In Morval, Cornwall, a limeburner was
paid 6s 6d (32p) per hundred bushels of lime burned in 1744. This must
have been an unpleasant job; the culm furnace within the kiln would
have been hot and dirty. The limestone was pushed through the top of
the kiln.

Lime was used mainly to improve the land, but sometimes for
building purposes. In South Devon, the chief source was the quarries to
the west and east of Plymouth, particularly the Cattedown quarries. In
Cornwall, by contrast, limestone was rare and sand was used as manure
instead.

The culm required for the furnace was the slack of anthracite coal. It
would have been brought by sea from Wales and landed here. This
could be quite a tricky operation, since the ship's master needed
precise judgment of the tides in order to beach his cargo.

Local Places of Interest
   21. Gateposts of Civilisation
   37. Hartland Church Seating Plan
Food and Accommodation
   Available in Hartland and Clovelly

51 A Charge of the Light Brigade Monument

Position: Hatherleigh
Ordnance Map: Okehampton and North Dartmoor Sheet 191 1:50,000
Map Ref: SS 5545/0455
Access: On the left-hand side of the road running out of Hatherleigh towards Monkokehampton: the monument is clearly visible just before the road forks, the right-hand fork leading to Exbourne.

Note: This monument on Hatherleigh Moor was erected by public subscription in 1860 to the memory of Lieutenant Colonel William Morris. Morris was a local man, born at Fishleigh in Hatherleigh in 1820. A soldier by profession, following the outbreak of war with Russia in 1854, he went out to the Crimea and assumed command of the 17th Lancers after their previous commander had died of cholera. On 25 October, he led his men into action in the Charge of the Light Brigade at the Battle of Balaklava.

Sir Robert White-Thomson, whose brother John Henry had been a

A detail from the Monument (see also the Frontispiece)

Lieutenant in the 17th Lancers at the time of his death at Balaklava, reckoned that 'Had Morris been in command of the five regiments composing the Light Brigade instead of only one of them, the issue of the Battle of Balaklava would have been more creditable to the leadership of that splendid Brigade, which would have charged to victory early in the day instead of to almost total annihilation later'. Sir Robert erected a frontage to the column in 1901.

Morris was luckier than John Henry Thomson at the Battle of Balaklava. Though twice rendered unconscious, he survived, being sent to Florence Nightingale's hospital at Scutari. However, he was to die at the age of only 38 at Poona, Bombay, in 1858; probably from sunstroke affecting the head injury received four years earlier at Balaklava. The monument depicts him being carried from the battlefield and was made by EB Stephens of London in 1860.

Local Places of Interest
    14. The White Bird of the Oxenhams, South Tawton
    15. St Mary's Chapel, South Zeal
    42. The Copstone, Copplestone
Food and Accommodation
    The George Hotel, Hatherleigh

The coat of arms, Frithelstock church

52 The Mason of Frithelstock

Position: The coat of arms is in Frithelstock church, at the back
opposite the main porch
Ordnance Map: Barnstaple and Ilfracombe Sheet 180 1:50,000
Map Ref: SS 4635/1955

Note: John Abbot (1639-1727) was a plaster-mason and from his will
we know that he owned a house and garden at the bottom of the hill in
Frithelstock. Not only does some of his work still survive, for instance,
the royal coat of arms in Frithelstock church illustrated opposite, but a
few of his possessions too which tell us about his way of living. His
wine-bottle, squat in shape, with his name moulded on the front, is now
in Exeter's Royal Albert Memorial Museum. His portrait is also there,
and the shirt he wears in the portrait, and some of his mason's tools.
His pattern-book, from which he derived some of his ideas for his
plaster-work, survives in Devon Record Office, Exeter. In his will, he
left to his wife Ruth 'all her Rings and wearing apparell, the moderate
use of one bed wherein she now layeth, two pair of sheets for her own
use' and £2, but in fact she died a few years before him.

The churchwardens' accounts for Frithelstock in 1676 record the
following payments for making the royal arms

'pd [paid] for lime and Cariage foure bushe and a halfe for the kinges
armes   4s 6d
pd James Lange for timber for the kings armes and for his worke about
them and the church   13s 6d
payd Phillip baudon for Nayles and spukes for the kinges armes   2s 4d
payd for hayre and squib for the kings Armes and for Cariage   2s 6d
pd for lead for the kings armes   1s
pd John Abbot for makeinge of the kinges Armes & writinge in the
Church & playsteringe of the Church and porch   £13 6 8d'

Local Places of Interest
   16. Medieval Wall painting, Weare Giffard
   69. Taddiport Chapel, Great Torrington
Food and Accommodation
   Available in Great Torrington

53 Shute Gatehouse

Position: Shute
Ordnance Map: Exeter, Sidmouth and surrounding area Sheet 192
1:50,000
Map Ref: SY 2550/9710
Access: Turn right off the A35T running from Wilmington to
Kilmington. Shute gatehouse is clearly visible from the road at the first
minor crossroads.

Note: The gatehouse was built sometime between 1550-70, and part of
the mansion it served originally has now disappeared. The initials WP
stand for William Pole, since the Pole family leased the estate from Sir
William Petre, Secretary of State to Queen Mary (reigned 1553-58).
Although in possession for centuries, the Poles did not succeed in
buying the estate until 1780; soon after, Sir John Pole pulled down part
of Shute Barton, and in 1787 built a new house, Shute House, farther
away.

The Pole family motto 'Pollet virtus' occurring on the gatehouse
means 'May virtue prevail'. Pole monuments are to be found in Shute
church.

Within the house above the fireplace in the Great Kitchen rests a
further curiosity: a spit specially made for roasting two oxen to
celebrate the coming of age of John Pole in 1829.

Local Places of Interest
    12. Loughwood Meeting House
    32. Colyton Octagonal lantern
    49. Axminster Carpet Factory
Food and Accommodation
    Available in Axminster

54 Arlington Granary

Position: Within the grounds of Arlington Court (National Trust property) near the stables
Ordnance Map: Barnstaple and Ilfracombe Sheet 180 1:50,000
Map Ref: SS 6145/4050

Note: This early 19th century granary in the grounds of Arlington Court has stood here since 1 November 1967. Previously, it formed part of the Dunsland House estate, in the parish of Bradford, a few miles to the north-east of Holsworthy. Dunsland was the home of the Bickford family from 1686-1817, after which it had several owners until taken over by the National Trust in 1954. The Trust made painstaking efforts to restore the house but in 1967, just before it was due to open to the public, it was burnt down.

This granary or cornstore is believed to be early 19th century, although similar examples dating back to the eighteenth century are to

be found in other parts of the country (the Weald and Downland Open Air Museum at Singleton in Sussex has several good examples). The grain would have been kept in wooden bins, and measured by using a bushel.

Local Places of Interest
    3. Musicians' gallery, Parracombe
  17. Spanish Merchants' House, Barnstaple
  58. Marwood Sun-Dial
  60. Queen Anne's Walk, Barnstaple

Food and Accommodation
    Available in Barnstaple: Royal and Fortescue Hotel

Bradworthy Well

55 Bradworthy Well

Position: In Bradworthy Square
Ordnance Map: Bude and Clovelly Sheet 190 1:50,000
Map Ref: SS 3245/1415

Note: A small stone building in the centre of the square at Bradworthy houses a water pump. A plaque attached to it records that it was 'Erected by public subscription to commemorate the diamond jubilee of her Majesty Queen Victoria By permission of the Lord of the Manor 1897'.

Bradworthy is believed to have been founded by the Saxons about 700 A.D. on the site of the spring, whose water is apparently very good. The attractive square is typical of Anglo-Saxon settlement.

Local Places of Interest
   50. Bucks Mills
   52. John Abbot of Frithelstock
   69. Taddiport Chapel
Food and Accommodation
   The Rose Tree, Bradworthy; Holsworthy

56 The Youthful Organist

Position: Exeter Cathedral, 5th monument on the left-hand side after entering by the North Door
Ordnance Map: Exeter, Sidmouth and surrounding area Sheet 192 1:50,000
Map Ref: SX 9210/9255

Note: Very little is known about Matthew Godwin, the youthful organist whose plaque lies on the North wall of Exeter Cathedral. Dying on 12 January 1586 at the age of seventeen years five months, he must have been born in 1569, but where is unknown. It is possible that he was related to Thomas Godwin, Dean of Canterbury, 1566-84. He was appointed in January 1584, two years before his death, as organist and master of the children jointly with Mr William Selby, whose assistant he may have been. Within six months, he had succeeded Selby due to the latter's death, and in July 1585, he was granted the degree of Bachelor of Music at Oxford University. Since he claimed at that date to have spent twelve years in the study of music, he may have been a chorister, although Anthony à Wood noted 'Whether he hath published any matters relating to the fac(ult)y of music, I know not'.

Local Places of Interest
    35. The Punctual Miller, Exeter
    36. Exeter's Medieval Aqueducts
    46. Exeter Catacombs
Food and Accommodation
    Plenty in Exeter. Cooling's Wine Bar, Gandy Street

57 The Spanish Tithe Barn, Torquay

Position: In the grounds of Torre Abbey in the centre of Torquay
Ordnance Map: Torbay and South Dartmoor Sheet 202 1:50,000
Map Ref: SX 9075/6375
Note: The tithe barn was probably built about 1196, but it is referred to
as 'Spanish' because the crew of 397 men from the *Nuestra Senora del
Rosario*, a ship involved in the Spanish Armada, was captured by Sir
Francis Drake and imprisoned here in 1588.

The *Nuestra Senora del Rosario* was the flagship of the Andalusian
squadron under the command of Don Pedro de Valdes, an aristocrat.
At times his advice had conflicted with that of the Duke of Medina
Sidonia, who was in overall command of the Armada. The fact that
Don Pedro's ship was abandoned by the rest of the Spanish fleet
immediately before the capture was to lead to criticism of Medina
Sidonia by Philip II after the remnant of the fleet returned home. What
happened was that on Sunday 31 July 1588 the ship collided with
another, the *Santa Catalina*, and was badly damaged. Drake's taking of
the ship without a shot being fired was not popular with some of his
English colleagues, who would no doubt like to have done the same
themselves but feared being reprimanded for deserting the English
fleet! The *Nuestra Senora del Rosario* was a valuable prize because she
contained the royal money chest. Sir George Cary of Cockington, one
of the local gentry, was responsible for the prisoners' keep. Later, the
crew was split up into three groups; five were sent to Exeter prison, 226
to the Bridewell, and 166 to Dartmouth.

A 'tithe' means a tenth part of the annual production of crops and
stock which was formerly paid once a year to support the clergy, not
always with a very good grace. At first, this was paid in kind, but later
commuted to a money payment because of the problems caused (how
do you halve a live pig?). The tithe barn was where the parson's tithe
corn was stored. This tithe barn had very wide doorways so that wagons
could pass through. The barn was moved to its present site in June
1932.

Local Places of Interest
 4. Puritans' Pit, Bradley Woods
45. Gatehouse to Cornworthy Priory
67. Galmpton Warborough Windmill
72. Oldway, Paignton
78. Brunel's Pumping Station, Torquay
Food and Accommodation
 Plenty available in Torquay

58 A Cosmopolitan Sun-Dial

Position: On the facade of Marwood church porch
Ordnance Map: Barnstaple and Ilfracombe Sheet 180 1:50,000
Map Ref: SS 5440/3755

Note: The sun-dial above the porch at Marwood church was made by
John Berry, yeoman of Marwood, in 1762. It is unusual in that it shows
not only Marwood, but Jerusalem, several of the 18th century
European capitals such as Paris, Vienna, St Petersburg, Berlin, Madrid
and places even farther afield such as Tenerife in the Canary Islands,
Surat in India, Port Royal – a British naval base in Jamaica – and Fort
St George, a trading station in the East Indies. Together with his son
Thomas, John Berry produced about twelve similar sun-dials for
churches in North Devon. Another good surviving example is at
Tawstock church.

The choice of places illustrates the struggle for Empire between
France and Britain at this date. The major European wars between the
two countries during this period involved colonies much farther afield,
the two countries pitting their strength against each other to win
control of these valuable possessions.

Local Places of Interest
  17. Spanish Merchants' House, Barnstaple
  54. Arlington Granary
  60. Queen Anne's Walk, Barnstaple
  76. Tawstock Gatehouse
Food and Accommodation
  Plenty in Barnstaple: Royal and Fortescue Hotel

59 Mohun's Ottery Gatehouse

Position: Luppitt
Ordnance Map: Exeter, Sidmouth and surrounding area Sheet 192
1:50,000
Map Ref: SY 1885/0560
Access: Take the A30 out of Honiton, turn first left towards Luppitt;
take the right-hand fork after the bridge, and the right-hand fork at the
next junction. Park the car near Pound Farm and walk down the track
to Mohun's Ottery. Mohun's Ottery is privately owned, but the owner
has kindly given permission for visitors to look at the outside of the
gatehouse.

Note: Mohun's Ottery was the home of the Carew family for many
generations. It became theirs by the marriage of Eleanor, a co-heiress
of Sir William Mohun (who died in 1280) to John Baron Carew.
Carews played their part on the battlefields of Agincourt and Bosworth
Field, and Sir John Carew went down in the sinking of the *Mary Rose*
on 19 July 1545.

   One of the most lively members of the family was Peter, the younger
son of Sir William Carew, who was a boy in the 1520's. His father
thinking this child 'very pert and forward' at the age of 12, decided to
send him to Exeter grammar-school. Peter, however, disliked school,
and frequently played truant. The schoolmaster complained to the
owner of Peter's lodgings in Exeter, who went to look for him 'And,
among many times thus seeking him, it happened that he found him

about the walls of the said city, and he, running to take him, the boy climbed up upon the top of one of the highest garrets of a turret of the said wall, and would not, for any request, come down, saying moreover to his host that if he did press too fast upon him he would surely cast himself down headlong over the wall; and then, saith he, "I shall break my neck and thou shalt be hanged, because thou makest me to leap down"'. His lodging-master reported this conversation to Peter's father, who came to fetch him and put him on a lead like a dog, and entrusted him to one of his servants to be led round Exeter in that fashion. Then they took him home to Mohun's Ottery, still on the lead, and attached him to one of the dogs for a while.

Sir William then decided to send his son to St Paul's school in London, but Peter liked this no more than Exeter grammar-school, so he was removed and sent as a page to a friend of his father serving at the French court. Peter served on the French side in the power struggle between King Francis I of France and the Emperor Charles V, but when the French did badly, he decamped to the Emperor. Here he was much admired by the Princess, but missed his family and friends so much that he persuaded her to send him home in style with 'a chain of gold about his neck, and store of money in his purse'. Having first paid his respects to King Henry VIII at Greenwich, Peter went back to Mohun's Ottery to surprise his parents who had not seen him for six years and assumed he was dead.

Local Places of Interest
   9. Plaque to Murder of William Blackmore, Clayhidon
  10. Tom Putt's Beech Avenue, Gittisham
  12. Loughwood Meeting-House, Dalwood
Food and Accommodation
   The White Cottage Restaurant, Honiton or in the town

Queen Anne's Walk, Barnstaple

60 Queen Anne's Walk

Position: Barnstaple
Ordnance Map: Barnstaple and Ilfracombe Sheet 180 1:50,000
Map Ref: SS 5569/3310
Access: From the town side of Barnstaple Bridge, facing towards the town, take the street on your left, passing the Bus station further along on your left. Queen Anne's Walk is just behind.

Note: Though now called Queen Anne's walk, it is probable that there was a Merchants' Walk on this site considerably earlier since a deed of Charles II's reign (1660-85) refers to it. The Exchange, where the merchants of the town met to do business, was rebuilt in 1708-13 by the town worthies ('viri ornatissimi') and the statue of Queen Anne probably presented by the Rolle family of Stevenstone (in the parish of St Giles in the Wood). The Tome stone in the colonnade was apparently regarded as a symbol of good faith: a merchant concluding a bargain would put his money there to show that he was in earnest. Garlands and the coats of arms of those who contributed to the building decorate the parapet of the colonnade which is composed of elegant Tuscan columns.

In any Elizabethan seaport, the Great Quay would be a focal point for the life of the town. A plaque records that 'in 1588 there sailed [from here] five of the six ships from North Devon which joined Sir Francis Drake's fleet at Plymouth and helped to defeat the Spanish Armada. The five ships were furnished by this town and their names were the *Dudley*, the *God save Her*, the *Tiger*, the *John of Barnstaple*, and the *Unicorn* or the *Prudence*'.

Local Places of Interest
   17. Spanish Merchants' House, Barnstaple
   54. Arlington Granary
   58. Marwood Sun-Dial
   76. Tawstock Gatehouse
Food and Accommodation
   Royal and Fortescue Hotel, Barnstaple

61 A Dartmoor Letter-box

Position: Ducks' Pool
Ordnance Map: Torbay and South Dartmoor Sheet 202 1:50,000
Map Ref: SX 6260/6790
Access: From Yelverton by way of Sheepstor village [NB: this should only be attempted by experienced hill walkers]. Follow the road through the village past Collyton Farm and Nattor to Burcombe Ford near Gutter Tor. At the ford, the road ends at a small car park, beyond which vehicles may not be driven. Follow the ascending Eylesbarrow mine track to the point where it forks at about one mile from Burcombe Ford. The left branch leads to Nun's Cross, the right branch descends to Plym Ford. Take the right branch, cross Plym Ford and climb the hill to the cairn on Great Gnats' Head. Ducks' Pool lies in a depression just over half a mile east of Great Gnats' Head.

Alternatively, Ducks' Pool may be reached from Yelverton by taking the Whiteworks' road at Princetown and then following the southward track past Nun's Cross for about 1 mile. Take the track to Plym Ford, thence on to Great Gnats' Head and Ducks' Pool as described above.

Note: Duck's Pool now contains no water but is a remote hollow in the midst of a fen. It is so called because of the variety of wild-fowl which once inhabited it.

In 1938 Dobson's Moormen, a group of walkers which had begun in the early 20th century as the Ford Wesleyan Recreation Club, erected a bronze tablet in memory of William Crossing 'author of many inspiring books on Dartmoor, whose Guide is a source of invaluable information to all lovers of the Moor'.

Crossing had died ten years earlier on 3 September 1928, virtually a pauper. Born in Plymouth, he first got to know Dartmoor through holidays spent on Roborough Moor, later in adult life living at South Brent, Brent Tor and Mary Tavy. A prolific writer, his accumulated store of information on the Moor was burnt four years before his death by the maid tidying his room because they had been nibbled by mice.

In 1938 there was only one other Dartmoor letter-box, at Cranmere Pool. Dr J W Malim of Torquay put the canister together with the stamp and tablet at Duck's Pool. Pens for the use of visitors to the Pool are also kept inside the box, and visitors' books dating back to 1938 can be consulted in the Local Studies Library, in Plymouth Central Library.

Local Places of Interest
Food and Accommodation
Available at Princetown

The Bath House, Ilfracombe (see overleaf)

62 The Bath House

Position: North-west Ilfracombe near Tunnel Beach
Ordnance Map: Barnstaple and Ilfracombe Sheet 180 1:50,000
Map Ref: SS 5155/4765
Access: From Holy Trinity church, turn left down Osborne road, then right into Torrs Park Road. Follow the road until you come to the Bath House on your left-hand side.

Note: The Tunnel Baths were built in 1836 by the Ilfracombe Sea Bathing Company, an organization which included various notables of the town such as Thomas Stabb, a surgeon, and John Banfield, a bookseller. The Greek Doric entrance shown above lay in front of tunnels cut into the hillside giving onto two beaches, the western one for men and the eastern one for women. Mrs Trollope in Colburn's *New Monthly* wrote enthusiastically if a trifle coyly, 'At Ilfracombe there is a deeply sheltered cove of exquisite beauty, looking so sacredly apart that it is impossible to enter it without feeling that Diana and her dainty train might there indulge in playing with the cool clear waves for ever, without fearing any audacious hunter's eye or fisher's either . . . And here in all the mystery of deepest solitude, the daughters of England having once, twice, thrice perhaps kissed their native guardian, retreated with shy step and dripping drapery, each one to her solitary dressing-room, where scarcely a sister's eye is permitted to follow'. The baths were well-equipped with sea or fresh water.

Local Places of Interest
   54. Arlington Granary
   68. St Nicholas Chapel, Ilfracombe
Food and Accommodation
   The Crown Inn, West Down

For illustration see previous page

63 Drake's Leat

Position: The leat can be followed for much of its course from Burrator
dam across Roborough Down to the edge of Roborough village
Ordnance Map: Plymouth and Launceston Sheet 201 1:50,000
Map Ref: SX 5180/6510

Note: Though the leat or water channel built out of the river Meavy to
reach Plymouth is still called after Sir Francis Drake, the original idea
for it was not his but that of the Corporation. As early as 1559-60, the
need for a water supply to the town had been registered as urgent, both
for supplying ships in the harbour of Sutton Pool – 16th century
mariners might lose favourable winds if they had to waste time hunting
for fresh water – and when the town was sacked and burned.

The Plymouth Water Act was passed in 1585, and also made

provision to prevent sand from the tinworks and mines on Dartmoor from spoiling the water. This was later to become a bone of contention. The leat was completed by Drake in 1591, and to many contemporaries, his feat seemed little short of miraculous: one version ran that the water from the leat had followed his pony's tail. A map of the period records the distance covered 'From the Fyrst taking in of the river [Meavy], that is now brought into Plymouth (as it is carried everie waie to geat the vantage of the hilles) is by measure 27 miles after 1000 paces to a mile and fyve foot a pace'. In fact, the distance is nearer 17 miles.

At the very end of the 16th century, there were disputes between the tinners on Dartmoor and the townsmen of Plymouth, whose interests in the leat conflicted. William Parker, mayor of Plymouth in 1601, wrote plaintively to Lord Admiral Nottingham 'I beseech you to stand our friend in the Parliament house concerning our watercourse which Sir Francis Drake brought hither to Plymouth; for if our water be taken away, our town is not able to live, neither are her Majesty's nor her subjects' ships able to be supplied with water, nor her army to be so well fitted with bread and beer'!

Much of the leat is still walkable, particularly over Roborough Down.

Local Places of Interest
   23. Rajah Brooke of Sarawak, Sheepstor
   24. Lady Modyford's School, Buckland Monachorum
   38. Marchant's Cross, Meavy
   79. The Meavy Oak
Food and Accommodation
   The Skylark Inn, Clearbrook; Yelverton

64 Wheal Betsy

Position: Mary Tavy
Ordnance Map: Plymouth and Launceston Sheet 201 1:50,000
Map Ref: SX 5100/8140
Access: On the right-hand side of the A386 running from Mary Tavy in the direction of Okehampton. Wheal Betsy can be clearly seen from the road as the ground slopes down.

Note: Lead, copper, arsenic and silver have been variously mined at Wheal Betsy on Black Down on the edge of Dartmoor : on a dark day, it is aptly named. A snuff-box previously held in Plymouth City Museum and Art Gallery is made from silver mined here. The 110 fathom deep mine was probably originally opened in 1796-97 and continued working until 1877.

So active was this area in mining that in 1817 the Tavistock Canal was opened from Tavistock to the edge of Morwellham Quay in the upper reaches of the River Tamar. The Canal was also useful later for bringing coal to heat the mine. The mid-19th century was a golden age for Tavistock: over half the world's production of copper came from the two counties of Devon and Cornwall. Wheal or huel is Cornish for a mine.

Local Places of Interest
  26. Brentor Church tower
  27. The Magpie Squarson: Sabine Baring-Gould of Lewtrenchard
  29. Lydford Castle
Food and Accommodation
  Grandfather William's Restaurant, Mary Tavy

65 Dame Aggie Weston's Monument

Position: Weston Mill cemetery
Ordnance Map: Plymouth and Launceston Sheet 201 1:50,000
Map Ref: SX 4580/5740
Access: From Milehouse junction, take the Wolseley Road in the direction of Saltash; continue along here until you see signs for Weston Mill cemetery. Park car at the entrance. The monument is in the south-east corner of the cemetery facing the tarmac path.

Note: Agnes Elizabeth Weston was born in 1840, the daughter of a barrister. A formative influence was the Reverend James Fleming, and she became an evangelical Christian, speaking out against drink in public.

The seed of her life's work as founder of Sailors' Rests was sown in 1868 when she wrote to a sailor to give him moral support. Her letters were so popular that three years later they were printed monthly. In 1874, she was formally asked by a deputation from *HMS Dryad* if she would be prepared to begin a temperance house for sailors. After some hesitation, she and her friend Sophia Gertrude Wintz began this work. Here is her description from her autobiography *My life among Bluejackets,* published in 1909, of the first day the Rest opened.

'Monday 8th May 1876, dawned bright and beautiful, the servants and ourselves were up with the lark. But the coffee was only just hot, and the bread and butter and cakes scarcely cut, before there was a loud knocking outside, the doors swung back, and in they came with a rush, and for an hour the popular saying was true, that "one might have walked upon the men's heads" – sailors just going to catch their boats, dockyardsmen going to their work in the yard, policeman come in from their night's round, all glad to get a cup of hot tea, coffee or cocoa, and a roll or cake, and during the day there was but little cessation from the stir and bustle of the morning. All classes, especially those employed by the Government, came to buy, to eat, and to drink.

'I felt very strongly that there was one important point to be attained. Jack is proverbially a "shy bird", and is apt to give a very wide berth to any place where he thinks that he will be preached at, or made a teetotaller. The problem was difficult, but it had to be solved; he must be free to come and go as he liked, whether he was sober or drunk, whether he had a creed or no creed. As long as he belonged to the navy that was sufficient; our platform was broad, no one was to attack him in any way; if meetings were going on, he was free to attend them or stay

away. There was no subscribing membership; if he was a bluejacket of our navy, or any other navy, or a merchant seaman, or a soldier, the place was free to him; all that he paid for was his food, bed or bath'.

Local Places of Interest
   33. Albemarle Villas, Stoke Damerel
   34. Devonport Column
Food and Accommodation
   Plenty in Plymouth: Le Croquembouche, Mayflower Street for eating.

66 'My Dear Mother' Clock

Position: Buckland in the Moor church tower
Ordnance Map: Okehampton and North Dartmoor Sheet 191 1:50,000
Map Ref: SX 7205/7315

Note: This clock, which spells 'My dear Mother' reading clockwise
from 9 o'clock, was erected by William Whitley of Welstor, the same
man who had the tablets of stone carved on Buckland Beacon nearby
(Curiosity No 44). He donated the clock and three bells to the church in
1930 in memory of his mother.

Local Places of Interest
    44. Ten Commandments Stone, Buckland Beacon
    70. Jay's Grave, Manaton
Food and Accommodation
    Available in Ashburton

67 The Galmpton Warborough Windmill

Position: Galmpton Warborough Common
Ordnance Map: Torbay and South Dartmoor Sheet 202 1:50,000
Map Ref: SX 8890/5670
Access: Take the A379 from Torquay and Paignton or the A3022 ring-road to their junction at Windy Corner where you should turn right onto the Galmpton road. Park beside the common, and the windmill is a short distance away. It stands in private property but can be seen from close-to on the common.

Note: The Galmpton Warborough windmill was erected about 1810. It was operational until the 1880's, and might have been used for grinding corn or pumping water. Apparently, it was damaged by fire, though the limestone walls remain in good order as can be clearly seen from the common land. Its tower (it stands over 30 foot high at 221 feet above sea level) is the tallest of those still surviving.

Local Places of Interest
   7. Daymark, Dartmouth Harbour Entrance
 45. Gatehouse to Cornworthy Priory
 72. Oldway, Paignton
Food and Accommodation
   Available in Dartmouth and Torbay

68 St Nicholas Chapel

Position: Ilfracombe
Ordnance Map: Barnstaple and Ilfracombe Sheet 180 1:50,000
Map Ref: SS 5250/4790
Access: On Lantern Hill. There is a car-park (paying) near the harbour beneath the hill, from which access may be gained to walk up to the chapel.

Note: Chapels perched on headlands looking out to sea were a not unusual feature in the late Middle Ages. Fulfilling both a practical and a spiritual function, they were intended to guide and inspire passing sailors. Bishop Lacy's register includes an indulgence of 40 days granted on 29 September 1436 to pilgrims visiting the chapel or contributing to its upkeep. In the 16th century, the chapel above the harbour ('capellam Sancti Nicholai supra Portum Maris') had a beacon light, and the hill is still called Lantern Hill. The dedication to St Nicholas reminds us that he is patron saint of merchants and sailors among others. In the eighteenth century, the chapel was adapted to be a lighthouse. Earlier this century, a weekly newspaper was kept there for visitors to read in return for a small fee. The interior of the chapel is now closed, but the exterior can be inspected at close quarters if you climb the hill.

Local Places of Interest
   62. Bath House, Ilfracombe
Food and Accommodation
   The Crown Inn, West Down

69 Taddiport Chapel

Position: Due south of Great Torrington
Ordnance Map: Barnstaple and Ilfracombe Sheet 180 1:50,000
Map Ref: SS 4878/1865
Access: Take the B3227 towards Langtree out of Great Torrington.
Taddiport chapel lies just over the bridge across the River Torridge on
the right-hand side of the road.

Note: The name Taddiport is not very polite. 'Tadige' is Old English
for toad or frog, whilst 'port' means harbour or town, particularly
market town.

Near the bridge is a small chapel. This chapel or chantry of St Mary
Magdalen is first referred to in 1311, but there is no mention of the
leper hospital until the will of Thomas Reymond in 1418; he left it a
bequest of 4d. In 1554, Edward VI's ministers reported that there was
space for 3 people in the hospital, though only one occupant at that
time. The free chapel had been established so that a priest could
dispense mass and visit the sick. The parish of Clawton, south of
Holsworthy, made a payment of 3d in 1593, but by 1665 when it was
assigned to the town dignitaries and the church authorities of Little
Torrington, there were apparently no lepers there and had not been for
a while.

Note the Ten Commandments painted on the wall, and also the verse
from the 2nd chapter of Micah 'Woe to them that devise iniquity and
work evill upon theyre [their] beds: when morning is come they
practise it, and cause it in the power of theyre hand. And they covet
fields and take them by violence, and howses [houses] and take them
away; soe, they oppress a man and his howse, even a man and his
heritage'. It is thought that this may have been put there because
someone had not played fair over the chapel lands.

Services are still held in this little chapel which has been in use since
the fourteenth century.

Local Places of Interest
  16. Medieval Wall Painting, Weare Giffard
  30. Bideford bridge
  52. John Abbot of Frithelstock
Food and Accommodation
  Available in Great Torrington

70 Kitty Jay's Grave

Position: Manaton
Ordnance Map: Okehampton and North Dartmoor Sheet 191 1:50,000
Map Ref: SX 7325/7990
Access: From Manaton village, take the B3344 running west. Take the second minor road to your left over Cripdon Down. Jay's Grave is on the right-hand side: a small unmarked mound in front of a wooden gate leading to a track.

Note: Kitty Jay was a young maid at nearby Canna Farm who hanged herself in an outbuilding, probably because she was pregnant. Precise details about her death including the date are unknown, and a slightly conflicting account is given in Beatrice Chase's book *The Heart of the Moor*: 'Her was an orphan 'prentice from the workhouse, 'prenticed to Barracott Farm between Manaton and Heatree. One day, when her was quite young, her tooked a rope and went to the barn there on the Manaton road, and hanged herself from a beam. Her was quite dead when the farmer found her'.

About 1860, the grave was opened on the instructions of Mr James Bryant, and the skeleton of a young woman was found. The bones were reburied on the same site, and a touching feature is that flowers are always to be found on the grave, though no-one admits to putting them there. At one time it was customary for suicides to be buried at a crossroads, perhaps symbolizing the mental torment which had led to the event. Suicides were not supposed to be buried on consecrated ground.

Local Places of Interest
41. Moretonhampstead Almshouses
44. Ten Commandments Stone, Buckland Beacon
66. 'My Dear Mother' Clock, Buckland Church
Food and Accommodation
Available in Moretonhampstead or Bovey Tracey

71 Toll hut

Position: Yealmbridge
Ordnance Map: Torbay and South Dartmoor Sheet 202 1:50,000
Map Ref: SX 5930/5200
Access: On the A379 main road from Plymouth to Modbury. The toll-hut is on the left-hand side of the road at the point where a minor road running from Worston to Dunstone crosses the A379.

Note: Modbury Turnpike Trust opened in 1759, and this little hut made of mixed stone, mainly limestone, was probably built about 1824 in connection with a new road scheduled to run between Yealmpton and Ermington. Less than 200 yards away on the opposite side of the road is Yealmbridge toll-house, a hexagonal building with a board posted up

Toll charges

Coach and horses	1 shilling (5p)
horse and cart	5d
bullock	2d
pedestrian	1d

The system of turnpike roads dates from 1663 when a stretch of road

running from Wadesmill in Hertfordshire to Stilton in Huntingdonshire had gates erected at either end because wagons loaded with barley en route for the maltings were damaging the road so badly. Turnpikes or barriers were set up by private trusts on main roads or highways to prevent cattle or carts being driven through until the toll had been paid; the money collected was used for the upkeep of the road. Tolls were usually gathered at intervals of 3 to 4 miles.

The indented coastline around Plymouth meant that for centuries much transport had been by water rather than by land. The steep gradients of land routes in Devonshire also hindered easy communication.

The turnpike system eventually foundered in the 1860's-70's due to the advent of the railway, and most trusts were wound up by Parliament. At one time there had been over 1,000 trusts responsible for over 23,000 miles of road.

It is pleasant to record that, like so many of these curiosities, the toll-hut had fallen into disrepair, but was cleaned up due to the efforts of societies and a few determined individuals, in this case, the Council for the Protection of Rural England.

Local Places of Interest
   39. Adrian Swete's conduit, Modbury
   40. Old Mother Hubbard's cottage, Yealmpton
Food and Accommodation
   Available in Yealmpton or Modbury

72 'I Want A Big Wigwam . . .'

Position: Paignton
Ordnance Map: Torbay and South Dartmoor Sheet 202 1:50,000
Map Ref: SX 8880/6150
Access: Oldway Mansion and Park lie on the left-hand side of a minor road running parallel to the A379 from Galmpton Warborough to Torquay.
Note: When Isaac Merritt Singer wanted a new house, he told his architect "I want a big Wigwam and I shall name it 'The Wigwam'".

Isaac had been born in Pittstown, New York in 1811. His invention, the Singer Sewing Machine, was patented in 1851 and in the following twelve years before he retired he devised no fewer than 20 improvements for it. Despite losing a legal case for patent infringement in 1851-54, his company, I.M. Singer & Co, was so successful that this made little difference.

Isaac had bought the Fernham Estate at Paignton in 1871. Sadly, although the Riding and Exercising Pavilion (a round building with a movable wooden floor for children's parties, of which he was particularly fond) was finished in 1873, Isaac died in that year, two years before the completion of 'The Wigwam'.

Isaac's third son Paris Eugene had equally grandiose ideas. Admiring the ceiling by Louis XIV's painter Lebrun in the Galerie des Glaces at Versailles, he decided to copy it for the mansion his father had built, and arranged for his painter to climb up scaffolding to view the original at close quarters! Paris Eugene also installed a Grand Staircase and Gallery made of marble under another splendid ceiling, this time Italianate. As a result of his attentions over the years 1904-07, the house had 100 rooms and it is hardly surprising that he changed its name from The Wigwam to Oldway house.

Oldway has had a varied history since. During the First World War, it was a War Hospital for American Women. In 1929, it became a Country Club. In 1939, the RAF took it over as a training centre. In 1946, it was bought by Paignton Council, in whose hands it has remained since.

Local Places of Interest
  7. Daymark, Dartmouth Harbour Entrance
 45. Gatehouse to Cornworthy Priory
 67. Galmpton Warborough Windmill
Food and Accommodation
  Available in Torbay

73 Stowford Armour

Position: In Stowford church, suspended from the SE corner of the nave (the wall to your right as you enter through the main door)
Ordnance Map: Bude and Clovelly Sheet 190 1:50,000
Map Ref: SX 4330/8700

Note: The armour consists of a wooden gauntlet, a leather coat and a somewhat tattered pennon; at one time, there was also a wooden helmet, but this has now disappeared. The pennon bears the arms of Harris and Buller, indicating that it must once have hung above the tomb of Christopher Harris and his wife Mary Buller.

Christopher and Mary lived at Hayne in Stowford, the home of the Harris family since the sixteenth century. Christopher had inherited it from his brother William. Christopher and Mary both died young, as explained in the legend on their memorial at the west end of the church. Christopher was buried on 4 July 1718 aged 30 and his two children, Arthur and Mary, not long after. His poor wife Mary, the daughter of John Buller of Keverell in Cornwall, died on 26 August 1726 at the age of 33, having left provision in her will for this monument. Christopher is shown in Roman costume, Mary in classical robes. But their heads are too big, and their legs too short. Their two children, in swaddling clothes, are also included in the monument, whilst two cherubs sit at the top of the pediment.

Local Places of Interest
26. Brentor Church Tower
27. The Magpie Squarson: Sabine Baring-Gould at Lewtrenchard
29. Lydford Castle
64. Wheal Betsy, Mary Tavy

Food and Accommodation
Available in Lydford

74 Sandford School

Position: Centre of village
Ordnance Map: Okehampton and North Dartmoor Sheet 191 1:50,000
Map Ref: SS 8290/0260

Note: Sandford School was built on the model of a Greek Temple in 1825 by Sir Humphrey Phineas Davie of Creedy House, the 10th

baronet. Before it was built, an architectural model of the school was made, and this was later presented to the school by Sir Patrick Ferguson Davie. The names of some of the builders are given on the model: the mason, William Edwards, the carpenter, John Emes and the sculptor, John Kendall. Sir Humphrey gave each of these men a silver tea-pot engraved with the words 'A Token of Rememberance (sic) from Sir Humphrey P Davie Bart to . . . on the completion of Sandford Free School'.

A 'Free School' means a school in which learning is given without payment in return.

Local Places of Interest
   1. The Dowrich Ghost, Sandford
  42. The Copstone, Copplestone
Food and Accommodation
   Available in Crediton

75 Brick Cross

Position: Bicton
Ordnance Map: Exeter, Sidmouth and surrounding area Sheet 192
1:50,000
Map Ref: SY 0715/8535
Access: At the intersection where the A376 running from Newton
Poppleford to Budleigh Salterton crosses the road running from
Otterton (half a mile east) to Yettington.

Note: This rectangular brick pillar at Bicton with a granite cross at the
top was erected by Lady Rolle of Bicton in 1743. There is a separate
tablet on each of the four faces of the column reading as follows:
> 'Make us to go in the paths of thy Commandments for therein is our
> desire; Budley Littleham Exmouth'
> 'O that our ways were made so direct that we might keep Thy Statutes;
> Otterton Sidmouth Culliton AD 1743'
> 'O hold thou up our Goings in thy Paths that our Footsteps slip not;
> Bicton Ottery Honiton'
> 'Her ways are ways of Pleasantness and all her Paths are Peace;
> Woodbury Topsham Exeter'

The Otter Valley Association was instrumental in getting it restored in
1985.

Local Places of Interest
19. Joan Raleigh's Tomb, East Budleigh
28. A La Ronde, Exmouth
47. The Whistling Cock, Ottery St Mary
48. The Thorn Tree, Salcombe Regis
Food and Accommodation
Available in Budleigh Salterton and Sidmouth; Cannon Inn, Newton
Poppleford

76 Tawstock Gatehouse

Position: Tawstock
Ordnance Map: Barnstaple and Ilfracombe Sheet 180 1:50,000
Map Ref: SS 5545/3080
Access: Cross the bridge over the River Taw driving out of Barnstaple.
Take the first road on your left to Tawstock. At Tawstock, take the
lane on your left to the church. Tawstock Gatehouse is on your left just
after the entrance to St Michael's school.

Note: This gatehouse dated 1574 is the only surviving element of
Tawstock Court, home of the Bourchiers, Earls of Bath since 1536.
The house was destroyed by fire in 1787, and a new house rebuilt by Sir
Bourchier Wrey in the Gothic style popular at the end of the 18th
century; this 'new' house is now St Michael's school.

The Earls of Bath were a power in the land. In the late 16th century,
the then Earl of Bath was appointed Lord Lieutenant of Devon, and as
such had responsibility for mobilizing the county's defences against the
Armada. In 1594, he complained that the gentry were not pulling their
weight by contributing towards the fort then being built at Plymouth.
'We understand this matter is much neglected universally by the
gentlemen, merchants and rich sort of that country . . . by want
whereof the said fortification proceedeth very slowly'. He was also to
be disappointed nearer home when, in 1597, the borough of Barnstaple
chose as its second member of Parliament a person to whom he took
exception (the other member was the Earl's former tutor). He
considered this was not fitting, so a fresh election was held and a new
member of whom he approved elected.

Tawstock church in the park just beyond the gatehouse is a treasure
house and should not be missed. The Elizabethan State Pew which
belonged to the Earls of Bath is particularly intriguing.

Local Places of Interest
17. Spanish Merchants' House, Barnstaple
58. Marwood Sun-Dial
60. Queen Anne's Walk, Barnstaple
Food and Accommodation
Royal and Fortescue Hotel, Barnstaple

[119]

77 A Fireplace in Church

Position: Poltimore
Ordnance Map: Exeter, Sidmouth and surrounding area Sheet 192
1:50,000
Map Ref: SX 9655/9685
Access: The fireplace is in the gallery upstairs, on your right facing
towards the altar.

Note: The Bampfylde family have been at Poltimore since the reign of
Edward I (1272-1307). Its members have played a distinguished role
both nationally and locally as MPs for Devon, Tiverton and Exeter. Sir
John Bampfylde was the Parliamentarian Governor of Plymouth,
whilst his son Sir Copleston Bampfylde was influential at the
Restoration. The family were baronets from 1641 and barons from
1831.

An unusual feature, though by no means unknown elsewhere, is the
panelled Squire's pew in Poltimore church which has a late 17th-early
18th century fireplace. This was often the only form of heating until the
introduction of stoves; in Woodbury church, a chimney was made out
of the roodloft staircase.

The Bampfylde family seat lies just off the M5; two granite gateposts
stand at the entrance, one bearing a crest and dated 1681, the other a
coat of arms. Both are surmounted by balls.

Bampfylde family legend includes two interesting versions of a tale.
According to the first version, a young Poltimore was made the ward of
an important person living in another part of the country. This person
brought up the heir as his servant, later his huntsman, telling the world
at large that the young heir had gone on the Grand Tour. However, a
shrewd tenant on the Poltimore estate suspected what had happened,
searched for the heir and brought him back to Poltimore.

According to the second version, boy twins were born, and soon
after orphaned. One twin died and was buried, his brother pined and
died too. One of the trustees who stood to benefit as a result of the
deaths had an argument with his co-trustee, and was overheard by a
servant, who reported the conversation to a magistrate. The family
vault was opened, but only one twin's remains found. Eventually the
surviving twin was found working as a gamekeeper on a Yorkshire
estate. He was brought back to Poltimore and thereafter known as
'Dick the Hunter' because he chose to live in a cottage rather than the
big house.

Local Places of Interest
35. The Punctual Miller: Matthew the Miller Clock, Exeter
36. Exeter's Medieval Aqueducts
46. Exeter Catacombs
56. Plaque to Matthew Godwin, Exeter Cathedral
Food and Accommodation
Plenty in Exeter: Cooling's Wine Bar

78 Brunel's Pumping Station

Position: Torre, Torquay
Ordnance Map: Torbay and South Dartmoor Sheet 202 1:50,000
Map Ref: SX 8985/6625
Access: Take the A380 from Newton Abbot into Torquay. The pumping station is on the left-hand side almost behind a cash and carry store soon after passing the Isolation Hospital on the outskirts of the town.

Note: What is an atmospheric railway? One which works by suction: the propulsive force of compressed air. The 'Atmospheric System' was invented by a couple of engineers called Clegg and Samuda who built a brief stretch of railway to demonstrate the principle. Although they did not receive much critical acclaim, one man who was impressed was Isambard Kingdom Brunel, the civil engineer. Brunel had been born in

1806, the son of another civil engineer, and whilst still in his twenties had been involved in the construction of the Thames Tunnel, designed the Clifton suspension bridge and become engineer to the Great Western Railway.

Brunel thought the atmospheric system might solve the problem of how to build the South Devon Railway between Exeter and Plymouth, where the gradients were steep. So in 1846-48 this system was built between Exeter and Totnes and on the Torquay branch. 'Atmospheric' trains began to run intermittently as far as Newton Abbot. But maintenance and other problems would not be overcome, and this station, one of twelve that had by then been built to house the pumps and boilers, never received its machinery before the project was abandoned in September 1848 having cost the company over £426,000.

This is the only pumping station building to survive intact. Its chimney in common with all the others has been made to look like a campanile. It is now used by a wholesale fruit merchant. Starcross Pumping Station (SX 9775/8175) is open as an atmospheric railway museum and the structure is complete except that the campanile chimney has had the top part removed.

Local Places of Interest
    4. Puritans' Pit, Bradley Woods
  45. Gatehouse to Cornworthy Priory
  67. Galmpton Warborough Windmill
  72. Oldway Mansion, Paignton
Food and Accommodation
    Plenty available in Torquay

79 The Meavy Oak

Position: Meavy Green, outside the church
Ordnance Map: Plymouth and Launceston Sheet 201 1:50,000
Map Ref: SX 5405/6725

Note: The oak at Meavy is very ancient; legend has it that it is a Gospel oak, sown when the church was founded, and there during the reign of King John (1199-1216). Sadly, it now has to be supported by artificial means. By tradition, the young girls of the village used to play skittles round it on Trinity Tuesday (a movable feast, since Trinity Sunday is dependent upon Easter but sometime between mid-May to late June). Their boyfriends paid a small fee for them to take part. Each girl had three throws, and she who scored highest would have the best prize which might be a new gown, bonnet or hat. A large tea was provided after the skittles, then dancing to the music of the violin whilst the men drank grog (a mixture of spirits, often rum, and water so called after Admiral Vernon who wore a grogram cloak) or beer, and the girls shrub (a drink prepared from orange, or lemon, sugar and rum).

The Royal Oak Inn near the oak is unusual in that it is still owned by the parish, although as we have seen (Curiosity No 18) at one time this was the norm rather than the exception. An entry in one of the Receivers' books (town account books) for Plymouth in 1589-90 records 'It[em] p[ai]d att the Church howsse of Mevye for wine and milke iis vid'. As we have seen, church ales were a useful way of raising money for the parish.

Local Places of Interest
   23. Rajah Brook of Sarawak
   38. Marchant's Cross, Meavy
   63. Drake's Leat, Clearbrook
Food and Accommodation
   The Royal Oak, Meavy; Yelverton

80 Staddon Fort

Position: The high ground to the east of Plymouth Sound
Ordnance Map: Plymouth and Launceston Sheet 201 1:50,000
Map Ref: SX 4960/5155
Access: Turn off the A379 running out of Plymouth at Elburton roundabout, and follow the signs to Hooe. At Hooe, drive up the hill towards Jennycliff Bay, and follow the road by the sea until you come to Staddon Heights Golf Club. Staddon Fort is directly opposite.

Note: Fort Staddon is one of the ring of coastal fortifications known as 'Palmerston's Follies'. A Royal Commission had been set up under him on 20 August 1859 'to consider the Defences of the United Kingdom'.
  Only a few years before, Britain, France, Sardinia and Turkey had united against Russia, whose designs on Turkey they feared. This was the outbreak of the Crimean War in 1854. But though France was an ally, the British government watched nervously as French 'ironclads', ships of war protected or covered with iron, lay moored in Cherbourg Harbour. Hence the need to fortify.
  One of the Commission's proposals was that two forts be built on Staddon Heights, the high ground on the eastern flank of Plymouth. Both look out to sea, but could also fire over land if necessary. Both have survived and been adapted to alternative uses. Fort Staddon is now a Ministry of Defence RN Wireless station and closed to the public, but you can walk round the exterior between the inner and outer walls.
  It has been much less altered than Fort Stamford, further west down the road towards Plymouth. This latter is now a country club.

Local Places of Interest
  22. Gunrow Signal Station, Noss Mayo
  39. Adrian Swete's Conduit, Modbury
  40. Old Mother Hubbard's Cottage, Yealmpton
  71. Toll-hut, Yealmbridge
Food and Accommodation
  Available in Plymouth or Modbury

Index